In Ned's Head

In Ned's Head

by Anders Jacobsson & Sören Olsson
translated by Kevin Read

ATHENEUM BOOKS FOR YOUNG READERS
New York London Toronto Sydney Singapore

Atheneum Books for Young Readers
An imprint of Simon & Schuster Children's Publishing Division
1230 Avenue of the Americas
New York, New York 10020

Book design and illustrations by Anne Scatto / PIXEL PRESS

The text of this book is set in Perpetua.

Printed in the United States of America

10 9 8 7 6 5 4 3 2 1

Library of Congress Cataloging-in-Publication Data
Olsson, Sören.
In Ned's head / by Sören Olsson and Anders Jacobsson ;
translated by Kevin Read.
p.   cm.
Summary: Eleven-year-old Ned, who prefers the name Treb,
uses his diary to record his wild thoughts about romance, school,
and the rest of his eventful life.
ISBN 0-689-83870-0
[1. Diaries—Fiction. 2. Schools—Fiction. 3. Humorous stories.]
I. Jacobsson, Anders. II. Read, Kevin. III. Title.
PZ7.O5217 In 2000
[Fic]—dc21   99-086169

FIRST EDITION

In Ned's Head

Death to whoever peeks in this diary.
May they burn in the fires
of doom forever . . . or at least
for a little while.

January 14

Guys aren't allowed to keep diaries. Just girls. You know, Barbie-pink ones with fluffy red hearts. My diary is blue. To make it extra tough, I drew a scary skull and crossbones on the cover.

First I thought I'd draw a brain, you know, instead of a girlie heart. But it just looked like six hot dogs stuck together. So I drew a skull and crossbones instead.

My name is a secret. I have the ugliest name in the world. It starts with an N and ends with a D. If you put an R before the D, it spells *nerd*. *Nerd* rhymes with *turd*. Luckily I have a code name. *Treb*.

When I write in my diary, I write Treb instead of my real name. Why can't people pick their own names? Then I'd name myself Sven or Ingvar or some other cool Viking name. Rambo wouldn't be so bad. Or Mister Vladinsky. Mr. Treb Vladinsky.

Our teacher says we have to read lots of books. She says books will make us intelligent. Wendy is the intelligentest one in our class. She's read about 9,227 books. No paperbacks.

These are the books I've read:

The Far Side Gallery

Green Eggs and Ham

Cowboy-Kurt

Cowboy-Kurt doesn't really count. I wrote it myself. It's about a cowboy named Kurt.

Every week our teacher makes us borrow books from the library. I just try to find the ones with the coolest covers. I never read them. But we have to borrow *something,* you know.

One time I picked up something from the wrong section. I thought I was done for. It was terrible.

Just as I was about to return my books, my teacher walked by. She stopped and looked at the titles.

"*Treb!* Do you read books like *that?*" she asked and pointed at a blue book.

It was by a Dr. Ruth somebody.

It must have been a pretty scary book. My teacher turned all red.

I had to do some quick thinking. I thought the book might be about how to get rid of headaches and backaches and stuff. So I said:

"I borrowed it for Dad. He's always wanted to learn how to do stuff like that."

My teacher gasped and stared at me.

The next day I found out what the book was really about. But I'm ABSOLUTELY NOT going to write it here!

I still haven't revealed how old I am. It's half-secret. But I'm not fifty-three or twenty-eight. I'm twenty years old. Almost. You just take away half of twenty and add one. Now you know, diary.

Spring semester has started. We're almost the biggest kids in the school. We get to act tough whenever we want to. Except when the seventh graders are out on the playground with us. Then we let them act tough.

Nugget smoked a cigarette during Christmas vacation. He told us about it in P.E.

"Now I'm not a little kid anymore," he whispered to me.

"Me neither," I whispered in my best Arnold Schwartzenegger voice. I said I'd actually been smoking quite a bit myself. At least seventy-six or so a day.

That shut Nugget up.

I've never smoked. Not even a filter. Except once when I was two I ate a cigarette. But I didn't want to say anything about that.

There are twenty-five kids in my class. I'm the third oldest. After Renee and Nugget. Nugget is going to turn twelve next week. Then he's going to try chewing tobacco. Nugget's real name is Nicholas. But I wouldn't recommend calling him that out loud, unless you're a teacher. If you do, you get a knuckle sandwich. You might get one anyway, even though you say *Nugget* the whole time. Nugget isn't particularly nice. But Nugget is the most important guy in our class. He's strongest, next oldest, he's smoked, he's most popular with the girls, and his dad has a red convertible Corvette.

My dad has an Opel that honks when you turn left. His name is Fred. I mean, not the Opel, but my dad. Dad is an optician. He sells glasses to four-eyed people.

Uh-oh, somebody's knocking on my door.

That was a close call.

Mom came in and wanted to know what I was doing.

"Reading comic books!" I screamed, and hid my diary under my pillow.

Moms are so typical! Whenever you're sitting quietly in your room, they think you're doing something you're not supposed to. Like lighting matches or sawing the legs off your bed or something.

Now where was I?

Oh yeah. My dad the glasses salesman.

Last Christmas he came home with a glass eye that he had to polish. Glass eyes are what people get when they're one-eyed. Then they don't have to wear a tough, cool pirate-patch. I put the glass eye in the fish tank to see what would happen. What happened was that Dad went running around the house looking for his glass eye.

"I've seen your eye," I said.

Dad was out of control. "Where!?"

"Right beside the other one."

Dad finally saw that the glass eye was in the fish tank.

"What the . . . " He almost used a bad word.

Dad has forbidden bad words in our apartment. It's a bad-word-free zone, he says. Except when *he* can't find something.

"Did you get water in your eye?" I asked politely when Dad was fishing his glass eye up out of the fish tank.

There are thirteen girls in our class and twelve boys. It's not fair. Whenever we vote on something the girls always win. Nugget says he should get two votes since he's strongest and next oldest.

Nugget says a lot of things. Like he says that those runts who are born after Easter should have to be in a separate class. Not sixth grade but fifth and a halfth grade.

We only have silly girls in our class. They're all horse-crazy and smell like barns without plumbing. All they do is talk about horses and how many times they've brushed Snowball. Snowball is their favorite horse.

We guys have made up a song. It goes like this:

Snowball is a super do-do

Yippitie-ippitie-dippitie-oh

Soon Snowball will only be

In a can in a dog-food factory.

Lisa is starting to get boobs. No kidding. They look hysterical. Like two oranges under her shirt. Or tangerines, maybe. Nugget always says:

"Hey, Lisa Plisa—where'd you get those bug bites?"

Lisa gets mad and tells the teacher.

Then Nugget runs out into the woods and hides for twenty-six minutes and throws pebbles at cars.

Now I'm going to switch to a red pen. Because now I'm going to write about something super extra secret.

REBECCA!

Rebecca is the prettiest name there is. I didn't think so three weeks ago. But I do now. Rebecca is the name of a girl in the other sixth-grade class, class 6B. She's the cutest girl I've ever seen. Even counting Arlene who lives upstairs from us. Rebecca doesn't smell like a barn. She smells like something nice. Maybe like a flower or that perfume stuff Mom sprays under her arms, or cotton candy.

Rebecca doesn't know I like her. I wouldn't tell her for all the chocolate in Hershey, Pennsylvania.

I've talked to her three times.

The first time I asked her what time it was.

She didn't know.

The second time she asked me what time it was.

I knew!

"Quarter to twelve," I answered nonchalantly.

"Already quarter to twelve?" she said. "How nice!"

Nice. She thought I was nice. The whole rest of the day I felt warm and fuzzy.

The third time I don't want to think about. It was out on the playground. Rebecca asked if she could shoot baskets with us. I was going to say YES.

"Ye—"

Then Nugget screamed.

"NOOO WAAYYYY!"

So I had to scream "NOOO WAAYYY!" too. I couldn't let the guys get suspicious.

Rebecca was sad. I was sadder. The last thing I wanted was to make Rebecca sad. I didn't know how to act. I absolutely couldn't go say I was sorry and kiss her on the hand. Then everyone would know.

Why did she have to ask? Dumb girl! She ruined everything!

Think if she hates me now. If she does, it's all Nugget's fault. It's not fair. There's not a girl on the planet who hates Nugget. Probably just because his dad has a red convertible Corvette.

I wish our Opel would turn into a Rolls-Royce with white doors, power windows, and a cellular fax. Then maybe Rebecca wouldn't hate me.

Bye-bye apple pie.

January 20

Hey diary!

It's Treb again. Dad just came in yelling and screaming bad words. I think it was a new record. He had
ripped out a hose under the hood of the car and couldn't
figure out where it went. I can't understand why Dad
always buys cars that break. Is it really that fun to fix
them?

Actually, Dad doesn't even fix our car. Mom does.
Mom is a bus driver and she knows everything about
cars. Dad doesn't know anything about cars. He only
knows how to break them.

Now I'm finished with my list of all the girls I've
ever kissed. My kiss-list. If you can really call it a list
since it only has two names on it.

Sharon and Raphaela. Raphaela's nose is so big that
you almost have to skip her mouth and kiss her ear.
Nugget says girls like to be kissed on the ear. He's
done it seven times, plus he always reminds me that
he French-kissed Geneva twice at the last class party.
He's lying. He only did it once and a half. By defini-
tion a French kiss has to be two minutes long. But
Nugget and Geneva only kissed for one minute and
forty-seven seconds. That doesn't count.

I don't know about this French kissing thing. I mean, there are normal kisses and there are dangerous kisses. Dangerous kisses are when you open your mouth and your *tongues* meet! It's true! It sounds disgusting.

Kissing Sharon is easier than kissing Raphaela. I guess she has a better kissing mouth and stronger muscles in her lips. She's nice, too. Raphaela isn't. Raphaela is going steady with Theobald.

Sharon suggested one day that we try a dangerous *French kiss*. I got one day to think it over.

I said no. I think I better wait a little with those.

Nugget has a long kiss-list. But I'll bet he made up the names at the end. There aren't any girls named Daphne Duck or Kay Onetwothree or Whoever Jackson.

Imagine the day I get to kiss Rebecca! Rebecca in class 6B. The prettiest name in the world. I'll bet I could kiss her for four minutes without stopping. But not a French kiss, you know.

I'm going to ask her to go steady with me. But first I have to find a trustworthy messenger. A messenger who isn't going to ask her to go steady with *him*. A good messenger who knows how to negotiate.

A good messenger is an ugly friend who asks a girl to go steady for you.

"Do you want to go steady with Moses?" the messenger is supposed to say.

Then the girl gets to fill in a box on a piece of paper. The YES box if you're lucky. The NO box if you're unlucky. And if your name is Moses the girl might not fill in anything at all. She might just laugh at your name. It's not easy having an ugly name. I know.

I used to go steady with Sharon. Our relationship lasted for three days. Everything was like normal except that I got to borrow her ID bracelet. And her library card. I didn't borrow any books with it.

One time Nugget went with four girls at the same time. Three voluntary and one involuntary.

Geneva, Louise, and Renee were voluntary. But not Barbara. Geneva made Nugget promise to go steady with Barbara, too, otherwise she'd break up with him.

One girl is enough for me. Rebecca.

Tomorrow Nugget is going to get a hickey. You can order them from Irene in seventh grade. It costs a quarter. I'm thinking about ordering one, too. In case Rebecca fills in the NO box. Then I'm going to show her the hickey. Then she'll know what she's been missing.

On Sunday I went to church with Mom and Grandma Marianne, Mom's mom. Grandma really likes church and God and the minister.

There are big windows in the church. Probably so God can check and see that everybody's there.

The church is really nice inside. Everything sparkles. When you're at church, you're not allowed to talk. Or to clap when the minister says something good. But you do get to sing. Church songs, not country or hip hop.

But you're definitely *not* supposed to laugh. So I wonder why eleven-year-old boys always get the giggles at the most absolutely worst times.

Like at church on Sunday.

It wasn't my fault. Really.

The minister started talking so fast that he almost turned blue. So I came up with a good little poem. It just popped into my head.

The minister turned blue
when he went to the zoo
and looked at his shoe
and found elephant doo-doo.

Maybe it doesn't sound that funny now. But it sure did on Sunday. I even thought he said *jammin'* instead of *a-men*.

Grandma got mad. "Now you won't go to Heaven," she whispered when I was giggling the hardest.

"I'm not going to Heaven," I said. "I'm going to the

hockey rink to play hockey." Because that's where I was going afterward.

I wonder if Jesus played hockey. I'll bet he would be the best. He could even practice during the summer, when the lakes weren't frozen over.

God seems to be a nice guy. I've never seen him. I think he has a beard. He does in all the books anyway.

Did you know, diary, that I have to count how many steps there are between every lamppost? Otherwise something terrible will happen. I'm not quite sure what it is. But I know I have to count them. I can't bear to think what might happen if I forgot.

I heard an awful rumor the other day. That Rebecca and Nugget are going together. Rebecca ♥ Nugget? Absolutely untrue!

Or is it? Maybe Rebecca saw Nugget's dad's red convertible Corvette and fell flat on her face with joy.

She can't have! I wish I was about twenty-seven years old and had my own red convertible Corvette. Then I'd drive back and forth in front of Rebecca's house and squeal the tires.

I usually ride by on my three-speed that doesn't have a back fender and whistle. It's super-scary. Think if Rebecca saw me and INVITED ME IN FOR A COKE AND SOME CHIPS!!! Think if one of the guys saw us. Me going to visit her. Think if I saw Nugget leaving Rebecca's house. . . .

I wonder if you get a ticket or have to go to jail if you run over somebody with your bike.

Nugget isn't interested in Rebecca. He's in love with Geneva. But Rebecca smiled at Nugget on Monday when his team won at volleyball. And in the cafeteria Rebecca brought Nugget a fork. It seems *suspicious*. Maybe it's time for private detective Treb Vladinsky, with a license to spy, to arrive on the scene.

Next week I'm going to ask Rebecca to go steady.

Bye-bye apple pie.

Howdy diary!

Treb Vladinsky is going to note a few important things.

IMPORTANT THING #1: Rebecca and Nugget aren't going together.

IMPORTANT THING #2: It's seventy-five yards between the lampposts in front of Rebecca's house. That can be good to know.

We have this thing at our school every year. It's called Fresh Air Day. We had it yesterday. It's like a whole day of P.E. out in the woods with free hot dogs. The idea is that we're supposed to learn to like outdoor winter sports. Like we don't already. But it's better than school. These were our choices:

go hiking in the snow

go cross-country skiing

go ice-skating

go home (if you had a cold)

The ones who went ice-skating got to take hockey sticks but no puck.

"What are we supposed to use the stick for then?" Joseph asked.

"To hit everybody over the head with," Nugget said.

Ice-skating is the best. But I chose cross-country skiing. Because a certain somebody else was also going cross-country skiing. I don't mean Nugget.

Parents had to volunteer to help out and drive us.

My dad volunteered. He had extra sick days at work that he had to use up. I thought it was great—until I found out that Nugget's dad was going to drive, too. Everyone wanted to ride in his red convertible Corvette. Nugget got to be in charge of the stereo.

Nobody wanted to ride in our Opel.

"My dad'll skid on the ice a lot," I suggested.

"Naawwww," everybody said.

Then I said that whoever wanted to could sit in the front seat and be in charge of *our* stereo. Even though it's not really a stereo. Just a radio. And all it gets is A.M.

Everyone refused to ride with us. Then I announced that, as a matter of fact, Nugget's dad had crashed three times and my dad only once.

"Naawww," everybody said.

"Meet an early death then, if that's what you want," I yelled and wished that Dad hadn't taken his stupid sick day.

At the place we went to cross-country ski, there are three different paths you can ski around. They are:

1 mile

2 miles

OR

5 disgusting miles

I decided to swoosh around the one-mile path and then eat hot dogs for the rest of the day. It went fine. Up until the end, that is.

Then I saw two people skiing along side by side. Nugget and Rebecca! I've never skied so fast in my whole life.

I'll show 'em, I thought, and I yelled, "Out of the way!"

But the only one who got out of the way was me. I went flying past both of them. KA-BOOM! I broke my pole and fell down head first right in front of Rebecca.

Nugget was laughing so hard I was afraid he might cough up his breakfast.

It took me ten minutes to get to the finish line with one pole.

"Look at Mr. Olympics," Nugget said and pointed at me.

"Gimme a hot dog," I said to the hot dog distributors.

But I didn't get a hot dog. I was forced to do one more lap.

"But my pole broke!" I screamed.

So I got to borrow one. One from the 1400s.

I went another mile—I thought. I made a wrong turn somewhere and ended up on the five-mile Path of Death.

I thought I was going to die the whole way. I even saw a hawk just waiting for me to collapse. Well, it might have been a crow.

Five hundred hours later I made it to the finish line. Everyone was eating hot dogs except the fourth-grade teacher who's on a diet.

"Well, I guess I've gone five miles then," I said kind of loud.

Nobody heard me so I said a little louder:

"Well, that's done then. It wasn't so bad skiing *five miles.*"

"Oh," Jasper said between bites.

I limped over to the hot dog distributors. "I think I'll have four hot dogs, since I skiied *five miles*."

I got one hot dog. That was all they had left.

I didn't see Rebecca anywhere. Nugget was sitting with the guys and bragging about how many hot dogs he'd eaten.

"I saw a hawk eating a moose," I said.

Then Nugget told everybody that his dad was probably going to buy a new red convertible Corvette this summer.

I wonder if there isn't a law against too many convertibles. Especially red ones. I'll have to look it up.

On the way home Arnold rode with us. He has two frogs named Rod and Todd. Once we stuffed Rod into Arnold's little sister's glass of milk.

"Look how lumpy the milk is," we said and laughed.

There were really three frogs in the beginning. Rod, Todd, and Dodd. We washed Dodd in bubble bath once to see if his spots would go away. They did—and Dodd, too.

Arnold and I do a lot of experiments.

One time we made a werewolf's potion. It was supposed to make whoever drank it turn into a werewolf. This is what we used:

2 cups Coca-Cola

1 cup black pepper

1 spoonful mustard

1/2 glass liquid detergent

1 pinch soil

4 crushed ants

Then we tried the potion on Arnold's little sister.

We decided to lock her in the closet. Werewolves can get pretty wild, you know.

She never got hair on her face. But she did get wild.

Not enough crushed ants in the potion, I guess.

Arnold is a good friend. He's worse at ice hockey, he's pretty weak, and his dad doesn't have a red convertible Corvette.

We've formed a club, Arnold and me. A discussion club. It doesn't work very well. I only want to discuss Rebecca and Arnold only wants to discuss Madelyn. Madelyn is Arnold's secret favorite girl.

Sometimes Arnold comes with me when I ride my bike by Rebecca's house.

Sometimes I go with Arnold when he rides his

bike by Madelyn's house. That's not as fun. It's uphill the whole way.

Arnold and I have invented our own country. It's called Hoppalochinia. Arnold was the president last week and I was the chief of police. In Hoppalochinia there aren't any red convertible Corvettes, any turnips, or any Fresh Air Days. We've drawn maps, made a flag, and written a national anthem. The flag is the best. It's blue with a cow in the middle.

I was supposed to ask Rebecca to go steady this week. But so far I keep messing everything up. So I'll wait.

In Hoppalochinia Arnold and I never mess anything up. We each live in our own condo with a terrace and with Madelyn and Rebecca. We have two choppers and a taxi to ride in. We catch thieves and assassins and throw bad guys in jail. The worstest bad guy of all is named Nougat. Clumpy Nougat. Why that's his name, I have no idea.

Now I'm going to go eat spaghetti. Think if spaghetti came in triangles and not in straight lines. It would look funny.

Bye-bye apple pie.

February 3

Dear diary!

Did you notice, diary? I made a mistake. Guys aren't allowed to write *Dear diary*. They have to write *Hey* or *Howdy* or something else tough.

I was sick today. Very sick. This morning I had a fever—ninety-eight degrees. You might not think that's much of a fever. I didn't think so either. I put the thermometer against a light bulb and presto! I was a dangerous 102.8.

I couldn't go to school today. I had to go on a secret mission, as Treb Vladinsky.

On Friday a special person is turning twelve. I bought a present that I'm going to send—anonymously.

That's right. Rebecca is turning twelve. But buying girl-presents doesn't go without risks. It can mean death, if your friends see you. The whole school might find out that Treb bought a silly girlie-thing. That's why I went shopping when everyone else was at school. This is how it went:

First I went to the grocery store. All they had were two plastic shovels and an eraser that smelled like strawberries. Then I walked by the perfume store three times.

I didn't go in, of course. Guys aren't allowed to buy perfume, just shampoo sometimes and soap. I thought I saw a sign that said: NO DOGS OR BOYS ALLOWED. Better not take any chances. I found the perfect present at Kmart. I walked around first to make sure nobody I knew was there. The coast was clear.

Then, there they were, right on the third shelf. The glittery pink notebooks.

Just when I was about to take one, I saw two high-school guys who looked like they were watching me. So I took . . . a pair of shoelaces instead. I'm going to send a note to Rebecca:

You were really supposed to get a pink notebook. But they were all out.

Signed: an unknown person

When I walked outside I ran into Iris Lindbloom. Iris Lindbloom knits blankets on Wednesdays with Grandma.

"Oh if it isn't little Treb," she said.

"Huh?" I answered.

"Treb, aren't you supposed to be at school?"

"Huh? Treb . . . ?" I said. "My name is Johnson and I'm thirty-seven years old. Bye."

I went home.

Arnold's mom is dead. She died when Arnold was eight. Arnold and I wonder where she spends her time nowadays.

"At the cemetery," Arnold says.

I don't believe him.

She floats around in the air and is invisible.

Grandma says that when you die you go to God.

"Where is *he,* then?" I always ask.

"Everywhere," Grandma explains. "God exists everywhere."

But he doesn't. I've looked under the bed, in the sugar bowl, and in Dad's Opel. I couldn't find him.

I wonder what kind of job God has. I know he doesn't work at the post office, anyway, because Atkins does. Atkins is always cursing and swearing and chewing tobacco. But I guess God doesn't need to work. He's done his job and now he's retired.

Arnold and I like to make prank calls.

One time we called an old lady named Ms. Abrahms.

We said her moped was ready.

"What moped?" the old lady asked.

"The one with high handlebars and red racing stripes."

"I don't have a moped," she yelled.

"Our papers say you do," Arnold said.

Arnold is good at lying.

The old lady was going to call the police. We hung up.

We like to call people with funny names, too. Here are some good ones:

"Is this the Fischer residence?"
"Yes."
"Caught anything good lately? HAHAHA."

"Mrs. Lowe?"
"Yes."
"We just called to say high!"

"Mr. Canon?"
"Yes."
"BOOM!"

The best thing to do is to call girls. But you have to watch out—it's *dangerous!* You can't say who you are. But you're allowed to give hints. Just like when I call Madelyn for Arnold. I say:

"Is Arnold there?"

"Arnold who?"

"Arnold Schwarzenegger."

Then we hang up.

We have a new neighbor. An old guy. He seems pretty suspicious somehow. He's about twenty-five years and a few months old. He has a mustache. He goes out at night sometimes. His name is Oliver Culver. That's a pretty shady-sounding name.

Arnold and I are going to spy on him to see if we can get the scoop. It could be good.

I think cheese balls taste better than cheddar on grilled cheese sandwiches. But Mom won't let me have cheese balls on my grilled cheese sandwiches.

These are things Mom won't let me have:

cheese balls on sandwiches

dirty feet

AND

holes in my underwear

Because think if I got run over by a car and had to go to the hospital. Then they'd see that I had holes in my underwear—a clear and direct sign of a careless mother.

Speaking of which. Sandwich. What a name! Think if it was called *dirt*-wich instead. And what do *witches* have to do with it anyway? Why not sand-*claus*, or sand-*deer*.

Deer are nice animals. They run around in the forest and eat grass. Then they get hit by cars. It's crazy. I want to have a deer of my own. Dreyfuss the deer. Then I'd ride Dreyfuss to school and he'd eat up all the metal off of Nugget's dad's red convertible Corvette. All the kids at school would get to ride on my deer. It'd cost a dollar. Except for Rebecca. For her it'd be free.

Bye-bye apple pie.

What's up, diary?!

Arnold almost died today. Not because he has a bad heart or anything. No, all the kids at school almost killed him.

This is what happened:

Arnold came running into P.E. this morning and announced that he had some hot news for the class. He said that a new kid was going to start at our school today. A guy. Nobody was interested.

"The guy's name is *Big* Eric," Arnold said.

Then everyone was interested. Arnold said that Big Eric was eighteen years old, that he'd been out at sea for a few years and that's why he had to repeat the sixth grade. Think if it was true! Big Eric would be the strongest person in the class. He'd be able to beat up everybody at the same time, even Nugget. What a dream! Nugget would be squashed flat as applesauce and I don't think Rebecca likes applesauce. Then the path would be clear for me. But think if Rebecca fell for Big Eric. . . .

"You don't have to worry," Arnold said. "Big Eric is already married. He lives in a condo with his wife.

He has his own laboratory where he and I are going to cook up new kinds of worms."

Arnold's story got more and more interesting. We found out that Big Eric could teach us all sorts of moves. You know, with girls. Not just how to hold hands but how to French kiss, with your *tongue!* Benny wanted to know if Big Eric was good at any sports. Arnold gave a chuckle. He said that Big Eric was a three-time national champion in most everything. Like soccer, for one. Benny was super-happy and thanked Arnold. Then Arnold told Theobald that Big Eric was a very talented bass tuba player. Theobald thanked Arnold. Theobald plays the flute. The two of them can go on tour together.

The girls wanted to know what Big Eric looked like. First Arnold said that the girls should sit down. When they were all sitting down, he told them that Big Eric had worked as a fashion model out at sea. He was always sunburned and had shiny white teeth. The girls almost cried with gratitude. They thanked Arnold with three hugs and one even gave him a half-kiss on the hand.

The only person who didn't thank Arnold was Nugget. He gave Arnold a bloody nose instead.

"That's the last bloody nose you'll ever be able to give anybody," Arnold hissed, "because soon Big Eric will be here."

The class all realized that Nugget's reign of terror was over. Now there would be peace on Earth.

"Big Eric would rather we didn't call him Big Eric," Arnold said.

"Of course not," we all said.

"He would rather be called Eric el Grande, since he's so good at Spanish. He's sailed in Spain and in twelve other countries. He can speak those languages, too."

Eric el Grande was supposed to start after lunch. Everybody sat at their desks and could hardly, scarcely, barely wait. Nugget was scared. I loved it.

Our teacher told us that we were going to have a new boy in our class.

"WE KNOW," we yelled.

"His name is Eric . . . "

"EL GRANDE!" we filled in.

The door opened. There was no Big Eric. There was a baby dwarf who was pretending to be a sixth-grade boy.

"Who are you?" I asked.

"My name is Eric," the dwarf said.

Then we all understood. Arnold had made it all up. Everyone was sad. Everyone except for Nugget. He laughed in a loud, terrible voice.

"HA HA HA! Look at little Eric. *Little* Eric!"

Now we have a new boy in our class. His name is

Little Eric and he's good at one thing. Getting teased. But before we started teasing him we tried to pull Arnold's ears off. We couldn't. He was too fast.

Nugget was fast, too. He hit everyone in the class on the back of the head in less than a minute. It was a new record.

Grandma is coming over tonight. She's bringing homemade food. I think I'm going to run away.

Nothing new on the Rebecca scene. I haven't seen her in two days. Maybe she's sick. If so, then I can be a doctor and make her better again. It'll be too bad if she's sick on her birthday.

The bus broke down when Mom was driving today. Some guy got mad and blamed it all on her. So Mom didn't fix the bus. On purpose. The guy had to walk.

Bye-bye apple pie.

Hey, diary.

Isthay isay Ebtray. Iay ovlay aay irlgay.

That wasn't English. It was a foreign language. Pig Latin. I'm bilingual, you see.

Last Friday you-know-who turned twelve.

I got her these really nice shoelaces, with two different colors and everything. I was planning to deliver them to Rebecca's house personally.

It wasn't easy.

First and foremost I had to make sure no one saw me.

Last and foremost I had to make sure Rebecca didn't see me.

I had heard that Rebecca was going to have a party at her house. I wasn't invited. I thought I'd put her present on the front steps. Then I'd ring the doorbell and run. It was a good plan. It almost worked.

I tiptoed toward her front door. My stomach was all turned upside down. Just as I got to the steps I heard voices coming up the street. I jumped behind some bushes. But . . . I'd dropped the shoelaces! Right on the front steps! My present to Rebecca.

Then a whole bunch of people came walking up.

They were strange-looking birthday-partiers. They were tall and old. One guy's whole face was wrinkled up. Another guy had a beard.

Maybe it's a masquerade, I thought.

It wasn't. It was all of Rebecca's relatives. One old lady was wearing an animal around her neck. Luckily no one saw my present on the steps.

I was happy. Rebecca wasn't having a party. She wasn't playing make-out games with a bunch of guys. It was just a little family gathering.

But suddenly an unidentified boy appeared. You know, one of those good-looking guys with moussed hair and linen pants. The unidentified boy rang the doorbell and then saw my present lying on the steps! He picked it up and gave it to Rebecca when she opened the door. My present! My shoelaces, with two different colors and everything. Found and snitched by an unidentified boy with moussed hair and linen pants. I was sure Rebecca was happy. Happy he came—Mousse-Head the Moron.

I stayed behind the bushes for about three and a half minutes. Then I went home and grieved.

Happy birthday anyway, Rebecca. I hope the shoelaces fit and that Mousse-Head the Moron didn't get any cake.

In two weeks it's my turn to turn twelve.

I've asked for a real fire truck with a siren. I won't get one. So I guess I just want a wristwatch that plays "Happy Birthday to You" and "Here Comes the Bride." That way I won't have to switch when I marry Rebecca in ten years.

On my birthday I'm going to have a party. A real party with girls and everything. I've already thought about who I'm going to invite. Raphaela and Sharon. And Madelyn, the one Arnold is in *amour* with.

That was another foreign language.

And Madelyn's best friend Nicole and my second cousin Beatrice. Beatrice always has to come to my birthday parties. And I always have to go to hers. It's something our wonderful mothers make us do. They're cousins. One last girl I'm going to invite is . . . Rebecca, of course. She's the one *I'm* in *amour* with. Arnold is first on the guy list. Then Little Eric. He's harmless. He's scared to death of girls. He thinks they're going to kidnap him and take him away to a country that only has girls in it. Little Eric doesn't want to go there. *I* might be able to imagine going. If I got to take my construction kit and a stop watch. Theobald is going to get an invitation, too. He's also harmless. He's going steady with Raphaela. Theobald's dad is from Iowa. But that's OK.

There's one big question mark. Nugget. Should he get to come or not?

If he doesn't, he'll get mad, and Nugget has a big fist. If he does get to come he'll run the whole party and dance every slow dance with Rebecca.

Think if Rebecca *makes* me invite Nugget. Or else she won't come. . . .

Maybe I won't have a party after all. . . .

I know what I'm getting from Arnold. He's already told me. First a thing he's invented with a lamp that lights up when you put two wires together.

Arnold says it's a time machine.

Then I get to be president *and* king at the same time for a whole week in our country Hoppalochinia. Arnold is nice.

My great-grandma Annette usually comes and pats me on the head on my birthday. But not this year. She's sick, Dad says. Great-grandma can speak French. Great-grandpa was from France.

"Merci beaucoup," Great-grandma says after dinner.

"Mercy buckets," I say.

Sometimes Great-grandma fixes us food. Luckily the food isn't as old as Great-grandma.

Great-grandma is funny. She says flapjack instead of pancake. And frankfurter instead of hot dog. That's what they said when Great-grandma was little.

I wonder why people keep changing the names of food so much. Think if they do it again in fifty years. French fries are called potato fingers. And spaghetti is called worm pudding. I know one kid who won't be eating anything anyway.

Bye-bye strudel pie.

Hello! Hello!

Treb Vladinsky from the planet Exus calling Earth and his diary. I'm going to come down now and catch a few earthlings. In about twenty seconds. Mostly girls. Over and out and all that.

Last Saturday I did something criminal. If anybody finds out, I'll probably get sent to jail.

Here, I'll tell you a little about it. But I'm going to use a code name for the thing we did. This is what happened: Nugget bought a pack of socks at the gas station. Arnold and I hid in a phone booth. We were squished. Then we went under the tunnel. Nugget took out a sock and lit it.

Nugget can smoke socks through his nose and blow sock rings. But he didn't feel like it right then. The sock made me cough.

"Only baby beginners get sock coughs," Nugget said.

"I got sock smoke in my throat," I said.

Arnold didn't want to sneak a sock. He's so nerdy sometimes.

"You know, you can get sock cancer," he said and left.

I smoked two socks, then I didn't feel too good.

On the way home I figured out that people can tell that you've been socking. You grow about three years older and get a wheezy voice.

When I got home I said to Mom in a wheezy voice:

"Hey Mom!"

"Don't you feel well?" she asked.

"I'm three years older. Can't you tell?"

"No," Mom said. "You look the same."

Then I went to my room and put together a puzzle.

Report on the recently moved-in twenty-five-years-and-a-few-months-old guy:

He drank a beer out on the sidewalk last Saturday.

Suspicious.

He had a black guitar case that could contain some sort of weapon.

Suspicious again.

Girls come to visit him at night.

They whistle all the way up, up, up the stairs.

Highly suspicious.

End of report.

I've made two decisions.

Decision #1: I'm not going to have a birthday party.

I'm going to have a *cocktail* party instead. Perfect, now that I'm more mature. Mom said we could have the apple cider with the bubbles in it. And we can put a cherry in everybody's glass. I've already sent out invitations. So far I've gotten answers from Arnold, Theobald, Raphaela, Little Eric, and unfortunately from my second cousin Beatrice.

Decision #2: Nugget can come if he wants to.

Rebecca hasn't answered yet. If she answers YES it's going to be a cocktail party à la hugging-and-French-kissing. If she answers NO, it's going to be a cocktail party à la punch-and-cake.

I think I'm getting horns. Something red and painful is growing on my forehead.

Mom says I'm just getting plain old acne.

I say I already have enough knees.

Mom says I'm starting to grow up.

It's true. At least my forehead is, anyway.

The ninth graders have cool zits all over their faces. They go around and brag about it.

Last night I had a dream. I dreamed about ears lying in an ocean listening. Then a seagull came and started nibbling on the ears. That's all I know.

I think I'll bring up my dream with Arnold in our discussion club.

39

Dad helped Aunt Lena and her hubby move yesterday. These are the things he dropped: a dresser, two chairs, some dishes, and a guinea pig. The guinea pig's name is Merle, or was, anyway. He disappeared under the steps.

Now I've found out who Mousse-Head the Moron is, the one who was over at Rebecca's. The stylish guy with linen pants and moussed hair. The miserable thief who snitched my shoelaces that Rebecca was supposed to get. It's Rebecca's cousin Leroy.

Leroy lives next to a highway. Lots of big trucks go by there. That's good.

I'm hanging on the brink of death. There are germs living somewhere in my room. They're poisonous germs that make you get sick. They hide during the day. When I turn out the light they creep out and try to infect me with diseases from all over the world. Like poisonous earwax and deadly morning eye-snot. That's why I have to keep my desk lamp on at night. The germs like sugar. I usually put sugar cubes in my homemade germ traps. I make the traps out of empty cereal boxes and a piece of string. If you put two matches on the front of a trap, it looks like a horse.

There are lots of things that are completely disgusting to eat. Puke-food. I've made a puke-list of unacceptable kinds of food. Here it is:

corned beef

Spam

stuffed cabbage rolls

mushrooms

Arnold's dad's oatmeal

Have you ever thought about the fact that the Earth is spinning in circles, diary? It's kind of fun, I think. I've done some experiments. I thought Dad's slippers might fly off the planet. So I nailed them to the living room floor to see if they'd stay. They did.

Then I glued the curtains to the wall. So they won't start flapping around if we start spinning *really* fast. That was a smart thing to do. Dad'll think so, too, when he finds out. Shouldn't you get dizzy with the Earth spinning like that? Another thing I'll have to bring up for discussion.

I heard a good joke yesterday. It was something about an old man and a tree that fell down a hill. There was something else, too. I don't really remember what it was. But it was funny.

You make ketchup from tomatoes. I wonder if you make mustard from bananas? Because it *is* yellow, you know. It'd look pretty stupid if you didn't mush up the tomatoes or the bananas. You'd have a banana on your hamburger and a tomato on your french fries.

Today I got a fat lip.

Bye-bye apple pie.

February 23

Listen here, diary. This is the last bleeping time I'm ever going to write in you.

Some stuff has happened.

STUFF 1. My cocktail party was a failure.

STUFF 2. Somebody peeked in my diary. In you, that is.

First, Stuff 1. The party on Saturday.

I got ready in good time. I was looking so cool, you wouldn't believe it. No one else did.

My guests: Arnold, Raphaela, Madelyn, Nicole, my second cousin Beatrice, Little Eric, Theobald, Nugget, and REBECCA.

Sharon couldn't come. She forgot to take her dog out. It did a #2 in Sharon's dad's briefcase. The briefcase had some extremely important papers in it. Smart dog.

Arnold arrived first, of course. He brought some firecrackers. Firecrackers aren't very dangerous . . . unless your name is Arnold. Arnold set the tablecloth on fire. It burned pretty well. Too well, Mom thought, and confiscated the rest of the firecrackers.

"Burning down the house isn't going to be one of the activities at your little birthday party," she said.

"*Cocktail* party!" Arnold and I screamed. "Not birthday party."

Then Arnold and I tried the invention he had made for me. A time machine. It's a board with a bulb that lights up when you touch two wires together. The bulb lit up for thirteen seconds. Then it exploded.

"It's a pretty sorry time machine," I said to Arnold.

"Don't you get it?" Arnold said. "We've been transported through time. We're in 1968."

We checked Mom out. In 1968 she was two years old. She must have been the biggest two-year-old on the planet. She was about as big as a grown-up. It all felt kind of creepy.

"Time to leave for the present," I whispered to Arnold. We left.

Then Madelyn and Nicole came. Madelyn had on lipstick.

When Arnold and I had finished laughing, I opened their presents. Arnold started laughing all over again, but not me. I had gotten a pair of ballet tights! Madelyn does jazz-ballet. She wants me to start, too. They need guys. You have to lift the girls up and be strong. Maybe the tights are kind of cool, I thought—until I tried them on the next day.

I looked like a hot dog. Can't you do ballet in a hockey uniform?

Arnold is in *amour* with Madelyn. He nagged and nagged until she kissed his cheek with her lipstick-lips.

"I don't think I'm ever going to take a shower again," Arnold said.

"Ridiculous," I snickered and pinned Arnold to the floor in front of the girls.

Then my dreadful second cousin Beatrice came.

"Hide the cake," Arnold said.

Beatrice and I give each other symbolic presents. It's something our mothers have decided. Symbolic presents are presents that cost as little as possible. I got a steel comb that looks like it's for a dog. Beatrice must have chosen it herself.

Arnold likes to tease Beatrice. She goes crazy. But Arnold is good at running away.

Beatrice is a man-hater. One time she hit some poor guy in the head with a brick. Then she forced some other poor guy to eat gravel. The first poor guy was Arnold. The other poor guy was me. We had pushed Beatrice into the water with her clothes on in front of a group of high-school guys. It was last summer at the pool.

Little Eric looked scared when he came in.

"Welcome," I said.

"I think I have to go home soon," Little Eric said.

Little Eric thought he had only been invited because there weren't enough guys. Dead wrong. He's perfect . . . can't dance and is too chicken to talk to the girls.

But he can sound like a whistle with his nose.

He gave me my present. Two plastic bananas. One was green and one was yellow.

"You can use them as swords, too," Little Eric informed me.

Theobald and Raphaela came together. They're a team. When you're a team you're allowed to kiss in public. On buses and playgrounds and stuff.

Theobald had his kazoo with him. He played "Happy Birthday to You" twice. When Theobald wanted to play it a third time, I put on a CD.

Then someone honked down on the street. It was Nugget and his dad. Unfortunately nobody had crashed into their red convertible Corvette.

Nugget came upstairs. "Howdy-do, party animals!" he roared so loud that Old Lady Andersen upstairs probably fell out of her rocking chair.

"Here you go," Nugget said and threw a present at me. There were two things in it. The first was a can of guppies. Two of them were dead. One was still alive—until yesterday. The other thing was an X-rated magazine!

The X-rated magazine was full of girls. At first it was pretty disgusting. Then it was kind of neat.

"Adults only," Nugget said, and held his hand over Little Eric's eyes. But he didn't have to. Little Eric had beat him to it.

Then only one guest was missing. Rebecca.

She showed up at 6:23 and 12 seconds. She had on a blue fur coat, two beautiful boots, and a bracelet.

My dearest diary. Are twelve-year-old boys allowed to faint in front of girls? I didn't think so. So I refrained.

"Many happy returns," Rebecca said.

"Thanks," I mumbled and she gave me a little present.

I felt pretty tough. It was the first time in my twelve-year-old life that I'd been given a present from a girl in a blue fur coat and two beautiful boots who wished me *many happy returns.*

"Yeah, happy birthday," Theobald said.

"You mean *many happy returns,*" I said importantly and squeezed Rebecca's present.

It had to be something romantic. A gold ring, or love poems, or a lock of Rebecca's silky hair.

It was a rubber snake. A red rubber snake.

"It's a wiener!" Nugget shouted.

Then there was a thud from Old Lady Andersen's upstairs.

"I'll bet the old duck passed out dead!" Nugget said, delighted.

Nugget asked Rebecca if my normal wiener wasn't good enough.

"Filthy pig-swine," Rebecca said.

I think Rebecca is going to be a writer when she grows up. She's very descriptive.

Then the catastrophe happened.

Nugget thought I was too chicken to poke Rebecca in the butt with the rubber snake. I didn't want to.

"Chi-chi-chi-chicken!" Nugget squawked.

"I don't care," I said.

"Chicken little baby," Nugget said.

When someone calls me a baby I just go crazy. I grabbed the rubber snake and poked Rebecca in the butt with it. I had a running jump. But it didn't hurt.

"Ow!" Rebecca said. "Disgusting."

Then she went home.

Mr. Diary. Rebecca spent 4 minutes and 26 and a

half seconds of her life in my apartment. Thanks to a rubber snake and an idiot named Nugget.

Now I'm going to Grandma Marianne's. I'll have to write the rest about my cocktail party later.

Bye-bye apple pie.

(9:46 P.M., Beep)

Good evening, diary.

I just finished brushing my teeth for the second time today. It's a good thing you don't have to brush your teeth with a broom. It would be kind of hard.

Now it's time for my second report on my unsuccessful cocktail party.

Rebecca left after 4 minutes and 26 and a half seconds. It was Nugget's fault. He tricked me into poking her in the butt with a rubber snake.

After Rebecca left, Nugget wanted to have a make-out contest.

Little Eric started crying and Beatrice screamed that she didn't know what making out meant.

"This is what it means," Nugget said, and threw my X-rated magazine at Beatrice.

Then Little Eric started crying even more.

Raphaela and Theobald started French kissing on the couch. Pretty dumb move by Theobald. His kazoo broke in half.

"Pretty nice, that kissing stuff," Arnold said, and tried to put his arm around Madelyn. But he put his hand on my cactus instead.

Now I *know* there's something wrong with Nugget. He was doing disgusting stuff with *Beatrice*. I didn't do anything disgusting with anybody. It was all too late. I walked around by myself and looked at all the couples. I had my hands in my pockets. So I'd look all sad and abandoned.

"Farewell, Rebecca," I mumbled.

Nicole tried to slow-dance with Little Eric. Probably for the last time. When the song got really romantic, Little Eric put his cheek up to Nicole's. To see, you know, if the light was green. Then he sneezed. Nicole got slime all over her face. Little Eric hid in the bathroom for seven minutes. Then he was OK again.

We ate cake. Nugget ate a candle. Theobald swiped the marzipan rose. There went his invitation for next year.

My grandma Marianne was born in Sweden. She says that if your piece of cake falls over on its side then you won't get married. It's true. We decided to try it out. I knew mine would fall over. Arnold spent three minutes trying to get his to stand up. I happened to shake the table, so now Arnold is going to be a bachelor, too.

Nugget squashed his piece of cake to see if there was any custard inside. There wasn't. Nugget said he had to take three more pieces, just to make sure.

51

Nicole's mom is divorced. Nicole put her piece of cake on its side on purpose so her mom wouldn't get jealous.

Little Eric dropped his piece on the floor. Then he choked on the next one and started crying again. It's his specialty. He's very good at it.

"Cry-baby," Nugget teased.

This is who's going to get married: Madelyn, Theobald, Raphaela, and Beatrice (poor guy!).

Then we had a cake war.

I was Jamaica and Nugget was Holland and Little Eric was sad.

"The U.N. is coming," Arnold screamed when Mom came in.

"What does U.N. mean?" Camilla asked.

"It means *you 'n'* me better get out of the way," Arnold said.

The war was over.

I got two lectures from Mom. It doesn't matter. Nobody loves me anyway.

We never played the kissing game. Raphaela had to go home and watch a movie. Theobald went with her and Little Eric got a headache, he said. But I think Little Eric had to go because his mom wouldn't let him stay out past seven.

"Thanks for the presents," I said and held up the

yellow and the green banana that Little Eric had given me.

Then Little Eric took the green one back.

"One's enough," he said.

It was after everybody had left that I noticed the world's most scariest thing. Somebody had read my diary! It was in *the wrong place* in my desk drawer. One of my guests must have taken a peek. A spy! It could be Beatrice. She's disgustingly curious about everything. She's always trying to find out secrets about everybody. It might be Arnold. That wouldn't be so bad. He knows my opinion on most things anyway.

If it's Nugget, it might be the end of me. He might sell what he read to a magazine. Everybody will find out what I've written. Nugget will spread the word around all over school that one of the guys keeps a diary. He'll put up pictures of me with the words: DIARY WRITER—HA HA! I know what I'll have to do. I'll have to scare Nugget into silence. Yeah, that's it. It won't be easy. He's strong and fast, and he has a lot of friends in high places. I could send him back to the Stone Age with my time machine. During the Stone Age there were dinosaurs and saber-toothed tigers. Perfect. I can kidnap him and force him to eat earthworms. I'll have to think of something good.

I went to Grandma Marianne's on Thursday.

"You really should join the Salvation Army, little Treb," she said.

"Actually, I'm a pacifist," I said.

Grandma gave me the New Testament for my birthday. It's the twelfth one in my collection. But I still haven't read it. I have to finish my latest Calvin and Hobbes book first.

Dad wanted to watch the hockey game on TV at Grandma's. Grandma said no. She wanted to sing psalms and hold me in her lap. She got half of what she wanted. Grandma sang out of tune. I went and sat behind the couch. Dad did, too, after four psalms. Mom and Grandma got mad and went into the kitchen. Then we watched the game.

I like sports. These are the sports I'm good at:

> soccer
>
> ice hockey
>
> darts
>
> AND
>
> push-ups

I've done twenty-four. Push-ups.

P.E. is fun. But not nearly as fun as afterward. Then the guys peek into the girls' dressing room. It's perfectly normal. The girls don't think so.

"Peeping Toms!" they scream.

"Tiny-tits!" we scream.

Lisa is the most interesting one to watch. She almost looks like Mom, except smaller. Sometimes the girls get tired of us.

"Look, then," they scream.

Then everyone is too chicken to look. Except Nugget. He gives out points.

I've figured out that eating fish is poisonous. You get cancer and your eyes hurt. I should go see a doctor. Some people say that fish make you intelligent. That's a lie. If it's true then how come the fish are dumb enough to eat worms and get stuck on a hook?

Our teacher says that spaghetti comes from China. That's the stupidest thing I've ever heard! Hasn't she ever heard of Italy? I think I'm going to go to the principal.

Bye-bye apple pie.

March 1

Hi there!

I'm going to become a rock star. It seems like a good job. All you have to do is shake your hair and sing a little. Then you get lots of money and girls. The girls will have to wait. The most important thing right now is to get as much cash as possible.

Our class is going to go on a school trip at the end of seventh grade. So we have to raise a bunch of money. If we get a million dollars we get to go to the moon. If we get $15.50 we get to go to the principal's office and explain what happened.

We're going to collect money for poor children. The ones at Bessemer Elementary School, class 6A. One good way to get money for the trip is to rob a bank. But you get two years in jail for robbing a bank, and the trip is only a year away. We'd miss all the fun stuff.

Nugget suggested that we sneak into the teachers' lounge and steal all the teachers' money. They're probably rich and have lots of money, Nugget said. Some of them even have *real* gold rings.

Louise thought that we should set up a kissing booth at the mall.

"Then we'll stay poor forever, as ugly as you are," laughed Nugget.

It was then that Arnold came up with his best idea ever. He said that we could become rock stars. Everybody in the class thought it was a good idea. Everyone wanted to be the lead singer. They didn't get to. Then everyone wanted to be the lead guitarist. They didn't get to do that either. We had a screaming contest. Whoever screamed the loudest got to be the lead singer. Nigel won.

Nugget said that Nigel had cheated. Nugget said he'd sung so loud once that he knocked over a wall. No one believed him.

Jasper got to be the lead guitarist. Because he knows somebody with an amp. Then we had a drum test. Everyone had to pound on their desks as fast as they could with their hands. Whoever pounded the hardest and could do it the longest was the best drummer. I won. Now I'm a rock-star drummer.

Little Eric got mad and said that, thank you very much, he could actually play a beat on the drums. It didn't matter.

Theobald wanted to be the band's flute player. He didn't get to. Flutes are nerdy. He got to play a single high-hat cymbal. Little Eric said that his dad had an accordion. Little Eric got to be in the band. If he can't borrow his dad's accordion, he's fired.

The rest of the class got to sing backup. They're supposed to be-bop in the background and clap their hands if the crowd hasn't figured out that the song is over. Nugget said he's going to clap out of synch. He's jealous because he couldn't scream louder than Nigel. Nugget asked if we wanted to ride to the gigs in his dad's red convertible Corvette.

"*Yeeaaahh, great idea!*" we cheered.

"Too bad you can't. I'm the only one who gets to ride in it!" Nugget roared.

The first thing we needed was a place to practice. Arnold asked his uncle if we could practice in his attic. Sure, his uncle said, as long as we each bought an ice cream every week from his Mini-Mart. Arnold promised. Theobald said that he didn't want to waste his money on ice cream. He doesn't even like ice cream. So I offered to eat his for him.

Our first practice went well. We lost half of our backup singers. They got a headache. Then we started to play. Then we lost the other half. Except for Sharon and Raphaela. They had earplugs. Now they're our choir girls. We have to wave at them so they know when they're supposed to take out their earplugs and choir.

We don't have a name yet, but we don't have any gigs yet either so it doesn't matter.

I think I'm pretty good at the drums already because I was the loudest of everybody.

Arnold doesn't know anything about music. He's only in the band because the whole thing was his idea. He calls himself the Boss. He thinks we should have Madelyn as a producer. I think that's a stupid idea. I told Arnold that you shouldn't mix business with pleasure.

As for me, I don't have any pleasures anymore. I'm alone in life. But if I become a rock star then girls will flock to me. Good.

Dad sold four pairs of glasses today. He's happy. They were all to the same old geezer who kept forgetting that he'd already bought a pair.

Mom said that Dad should be ashamed of himself. Dad said that forgetful people are good for the economy. Then he forgot where he'd put his wallet.

Think if there were purple beans instead of brown ones. I think they'd sell more then because purple is a cooler color.

Bye-bye apple pie.

The 18th of March, this year

Good-bye live-ary,

My name isn't Treb and I'm not twelve years old. I'm a girl and I have twenty-five brothers and a dad with a Corvette that can fly. My best friend's name isn't Arnold, but Schmarnold.

Did you notice, diary? I'm lying. It's something I have to do today. I'm sick. I'm lying in bed and I'm being attacked by sharks.

There's nothing else to do when you're sick except to lie. An hour ago I fought with two grizzly bears who live in a chestnut tree. The chestnut tree is in my closet. From a distance it looks like a pair of skis. But that's wrong.

I have the flu. The flu is a fever, a stomachache, and a headache all rolled up into one. How convenient.

"The flu usually passes in a day," Mom said.

Tomorrow we have a math test.

I don't think the flu usually passes until two days or so. A warning!

I knew last night that I was going to get sick. When I checked my germ-traps under my bed and behind my chair, I saw the horrible truth. Somebody had destroyed the traps. From the inside!

A giant germ. As big as a cereal box.

The germ-giant is green and has fourteen eyes.
Diseases you can get from the germ-giant:

the flu

the chicken pox

the plague

nearsightedness

It's a good thing I didn't get the plague. But there's something worse. *Nearsightedness*. Then you have to get glasses. That's dangerous.

No girl will get close to a guy with glasses.

No soccer team will pick a guy with glasses.

No friend will wrestle with a guy with glasses.

I have to capture the germ-giant before it infects me with nearsightedness.

I'm going to talk to Arnold about good capture methods. He's good at stuff like that.

Now my room is burning down. Fireman Treb Vladinsky dives heroically into the flames and saves about twelve people from a terrible death. The germ-giant gives an evil laugh from the closet. He's the culprit. But grizzly bears climb down from the chestnut tree and trample the germ to death.

Squish, squash, squ-uush, gone.

That was a good idea.

I'm going to call the zoo and ask if I can borrow a

bear who can walk around a little in my room and squish all the germs.

Theobald and I went puddle-jumping yesterday. It was fun.

Theobald's shoe came off and he blamed it on me.

Then we went home.

Theobald drank coffee. I did no such thing.

"Denture-making potion," I said, and drank a Coke instead.

Mom likes Theobald. Mostly because he drinks coffee and plays the flute.

Arnold drinks coffee, too. He likes to experiment with it. To check certain things. For example:

- How many sugar cubes fit in a full cup.

  Twenty-seven. But then there's no room for the coffee.

- How long it takes for different kinds of sugar cubes to dissolve in the coffee.

- How long it takes before Mom gets tired of Arnold's experiments.

  Three minutes and twelve seconds.

- If anyone would dare to drink coffee with food coloring and salt in it.

Dad dared. He thought it was a Malaysian margarita. He spit for 19.3 seconds when we told him the truth.

Think if you could lie on the ceiling and look up at the floor. Mom would be surprised.

We live in an apartment. This is who else lives in our building:

BOTTOM LEFT
Juan Bergstrom with his girlfriend. They have a daughter, unfortunately not twelve years old, but one and a half. Juan doesn't sleep at night.

One time he sang a song for me. It was beautiful. His girlfriend didn't think it was beautiful.

"Juan, you promised you wouldn't bother little kids when you've been drinking," she said.

BOTTOM RIGHT
The Captain. He's been in the military. He's funny. He likes to march with us by the swings.

"TEN-HUTT!" he screams until his whole face turns red.

"The Red Baron!" we scream.

"Captain!" he screams.

The Captain's apartment looks like a fort. He has pistols on the walls and two maps. When he vacuums he puts on his World War II helmet. Then he sings a song.

Dad says that the Captain has a few loose screws.

"Thank you," I say, "and the same to you."

MIDDLE LEFT

The Floyds. The father's name is Fritz and he's an optician. The mother's name is Madelaine and she's a bus driver.

They have a smart son. He's nice in every way. He's about twelve years old and has the flu. The at-least-two-day kind.

There's somebody else who lives there, too. Not really a person.

His name is the germ-giant.

MIDDLE RIGHT

A mysterious person. An old man around twenty-five who whistles in the stairwell.

One time he said: *"Hi!"*

I wonder what he meant by that.

His name is Oliver Culver. Weird name.

TOP LEFT

Old Lady Andersen. She's about 132 years old. She listens to everything. I guess she has big ears.

Old Lady Andersen has a home-care nurse who visits her twice a week. She rides a moped. The nurse, I mean. I thought it was against the law for adults to ride mopeds.

Mom feels sorry for Old Lady Andersen. She feels so sorry for her that she sends me upstairs with bread and muffins.

I hang the bag on the doorknob.

TOP RIGHT

The Fotzwits. Or half of them anyway. They got divorced last year. Papa Fotzwit and Arlene Fotzwit are left.

Arlene is fifteen. I think she's going to be a model. Papa Fotzwit works with computers. He's the only grown-up I know who knows how to play Mario Brothers right. They have two canaries who sing. I've never understood the words. Canary language is hard.

A wild grizzly bear is coming right at me with big

slobbery jaws. I better go, so I can hit him on the head a few times.

I have brown-and-white wallpaper.

Bye-bye apple pie.

The middle of week #16

(almost Easter)

Catastrophe, diary.

This must be my unluckiest year ever.

> PIECE OF UNLUCK #1: Rebecca doesn't love me.
>
> PIECE OF UNLUCK #2: Nugget's dad's red convertible Corvette is still in one piece.
>
> PIECE OF UNLUCK #3: I know that someone else has read my diary.

And the most unluckiest thing of all: the germ-giant has ruined me for life. I HAVE TO GET GLASSES! I'M GOING TO BE A FOUR-EYES! I'M GOING TO DIE!!!

First I got the flu from the germ-giant. Then I got nearsightedness.

Can't you get anything fun from that stupid germ?

Bad luck having a dad who's an optician. He's the one who figured out that I'm nearsighted.

I was squinting one night when we were watching TV.

"Aaaah," Dad said. "Examination."

He forced me to go to his store.

"I'm innocent, I'm innocent," I cried. I argued that I absolutely definitely wasn't nearsighted. Dad didn't believe me. I peeked at the chart when we walked in.

C Z R P O T L, it said all the way at the bottom.

Aha! I thought. C Z R P . . . I'll have to remember that.

"What's it say all the way at the bottom?" Dad asked.

"Piece of cake," I laughed. "C Z . . . V . . . G . . . Mmmmm . . . "

"No, not M," Dad said.

"It says A C R L P B L M H," I blurted out.

I lied. I couldn't see what it said. I couldn't remember either. I blurted on purpose. It was a good trick.

But not good enough. Dad didn't believe me. My plan had failed miserably and I had to go try on ugly disgusting frames. I wanted sunglasses.

"Forget it," Dad said. "Hey . . . "

"Hay is for horses," I said.

"Hey," he said, "these are pretty cool."

He pulled out a pair of bookworm glasses with a blue frame.

I fainted. (small lie)

I am now the unproud wearer of a pair of glasses. I'm not going to wear my glasses in public. Not even at school. Only when I watch TV. Then I'll close the curtains, of course.

Stupid germ-giant! I have to figure out some way to catch him.

I called the zoo and tried to rent a bear that could walk around our apartment and trample here and there, preferably right on my glasses. They hung up.

Then I thought maybe Arnold could help me.

But he's too scared to come over with the germ-giant on the loose. He doesn't want to be a four-eyes either.

I decided to get help from somebody who is already nearsighted. That should be risk-free.

Dade in seventh grade has glasses. He has spiked hair and checkered glasses and earrings. . . . Now that I think about it, he almost looks like a germ-giant.

The perfect bait.

Yesterday Canada beat us at ice hockey. Dad threw socks at the TV and tore up the *TV Guide*. He said he was going to get a tank and drive up to the border. I hope he's lying.

Now for the entertainment.

Mom and Dad are trying not to eat. It's called fasting. Ha ha! They're only allowed to drink vile juices and disgusting bouillon. These are sort of what they drink:

sawdust juice

beetle bouillon

mush punch

weed tea

sewer water

Dad is about to die. I teased him.

"Do you want a hot dog, Dad?"

"I think I'm going to go have a BLT, Dad."

"Do you want a piece of my pizza, Dad?"

And so on. And so on. And so on.

Finally they sent me to Grandma's. Right after I'd found a trail of bread crumbs in the bathroom.

"Dad's eating in the john," I whispered to Mom.

She didn't believe me. Now I'm at Grandma's. I'm going to be here until Easter.

Grandma wants me to paint Easter eggs. She says it's cute.

I say it's for babies. I'm grown-up this year.

I'll be in puberty soon. In puberty you get muscles and a deep voice. And a mustache and hair on your chest—after a while. It's going to be exciting. I think a mustache and muscles are just what I need.

I read some of the Bible for Grandma. I changed the story a little. I said Batman instead of Jesus. And Ponchus Penguin instead of Ponchus Pilot.

This is what I said: "And the applesauce took its apples from Egypt and departed for the pre-sauced land."

By then Grandma had fallen asleep. She snored.

I've discovered something on the balcony. There's a flat, empty box of cereal there. A germ trap! A germ-giant in Grandma's apartment, too. Maybe it's the same germ-giant that's chasing me. I might get the plague soon . . . from the germ-giant.

It's a good thing I brought Dad's fishing net. I have to be on my guard.

On Good Friday all of our relatives are coming over to Grandma's. Not Mom and Dad. They'll probably have eaten each other up by then.

The relatives who are coming:

Aunt Minora and Uncle Gustave. They live in a big house. They look rich.

"They're just bluffing," Dad says.

Sambob, Lester, and Sandra are their kids. They're all old and taller than skyscrapers. Sambob is twenty-one. Lester is nineteen. Sandra is seventeen.

Sandra is nice. She has a perfect face, flawless hair, and wonderful posture. Sandra looks very friendly. You're not allowed to think that cousins are hot-looking. That's why she looks friendly.

Sambob, Lester, and Sandra almost talk like Americans. They live in Texas. One time Lester threw a turtle at me to check my pain threshold. Sambob knows the names of all the capitals in the world. Lester isn't as good. He only knows the ones in North America and western Africa.

Grandma's sister Claire is coming, too. She's lived in Venezuela. She can say *burrito* faster than you can think it.

Then Uncle Ted and Aunt Rose are coming. With my two cousins Anna and Sofia.

I like to sing a song:

It's only a hunch—Ted sneezed up his lunch.

Anna and Sofia both have diarrhea.

And Aunt Rose just blows her nose.

Then I don't get any chocolate eggs.

I don't care. I'll eat real eggs. I'm going to eat twelve and a half on Easter day. The other half I'm going to use as bait for the germ-giant.

Bye-bye Easter pie.

Simsalabeem, diary.

First, some of my secret language:
Konkakloff siliboom putten treypee troff.
Everything is secret today. Arnold spent the night.
His dad is taking an evening class. He's learning how
to scream.

Arnold and I have a new job. We're magicians. We
practiced yesterday. We made the fish stew turn into
hamburgers. Mom caught us.

These are the things we made disappear:

Dad's reading glasses

Dad's car keys

Dad's linen pants

Dad's patience

These are the things we made appear:

Dad's rotten mood

bad words

a glass of water

a fire truck (almost)

Mom's headache. That was the easiest.

We had a show for Mom and Dad.

Arnold got a magician's kit for Christmas. It's mysterious.

You can bend the magic wand—one way. I bent it the other. . . .

It wasn't a very good magic wand anyway.

We practiced for a long time on this one trick with an orange. Then we got hungry and we ate the orange.

Arnold called himself the Invincible Dr. Sandwich. I had to use the name Smith.

"It is *my* magic kit," Arnold said.

Arnold safety-pinned a rubber band to the inside of his sleeve. Then he taped a ten-dollar bill to the other end of the rubber band. He showed the ten-dollar bill to the audience (Mom and Dad), but he kept the rubber band hidden.

"Ladies and gentlemen. The ten-dollar bill will now disappear."

It did. But not up his sleeve. It flew into the fish tank.

Dad laughed—until he found out that it was his ten-dollar bill.

The Invincible Dr. Sandwich blamed everything on Smith.

"Smith will have the sum removed from his pay-check," said the Invincible Dr. Sandwich.

Then Arnold juggled three apples. One became applesauce.

The audience applauded. Dad got up and wanted to do a card trick.

But the performance was over.

In two weeks from Friday I get my disgusting glasses. Everybody knows that it's not my fault. It's all because of the germ-giant that infected me with nearsightedness.

Arnold refused to come over last week. He didn't want to get bitten and turned into a four-eyes.

But Arnold is smart. He invented a medicine to protect him from the germ-giant. If you take the medicine you won't become nearsighted. So Arnold did. I asked him what was in it.

"It's a secret," Arnold said. "And scientists never reveal their secrets."

WARNING! The germ-giant is still uncaptured. But at night I can hear it scratching in the dark.

"Can't the Invincible Dr. Sandwich make the germ-giant magically disappear?" I asked Arnold before we went to sleep.

Arnold didn't know. But he said he'd try the next day.

After that, our discussion club had a meeting.

"This is a good opportunity to bring up the subject of girls," Arnold said.

Then he told me that things were looking pretty good with Madelyn. He said that he expected to start going steady with her sometime in May.

I didn't discuss the subject of girls much at all.

"Girls are stupid," was all I said.

"But what about Rebecca?" Arnold asked me.

"Now who was that again?" I asked. "Oh yeah. The one with eyebrows and dark hair. She's forgotten."

We talked about airplane wings for ten minutes.

"Good night, the Invincible Dr. Sandwich," I said.

"Good night, Assistant Smith," Arnold said.

"The Invincible Assistant Smith," I said.

The Invincible Assistant Smith was instantly fast asleep.

I was dreaming something about Treb Vladinsky's latest mission. Treb Vladinsky was fighting off seven ninjas.

Suddenly somebody was poking me in the stomach. I woke up.

"How do you fall asleep?" Arnold asked me. He said that he wanted to take a survey.

I had to tell him everything. This is what I said:

1. I lie down.

2. I close my eyes.

3. I relax.

4. I think about good things. Cartoons and stuff.

5. I don't think about bad things like germ-giants, glasses, or Nugget.

6. I fall asleep.

"Understand?" I asked.

He didn't. He was asleep.

We did more magic tricks when we got up. First we wanted to make water magically appear in the TV to see if the kids' shows were waterproof. Mom kicked us out. We went out to the playground. The Captain was sitting there on a bench.

"We're magicians," we said.

"Good, magician me a woman," said the Captain.

We couldn't.

"Then magician me the helmet I lost," he asked.

We couldn't.

"What *can* you do then?" the Captain howled.

"We can make you invisible," Arnold said.

Arnold is crazy.

"Hocus pocus, peepeeyokus, now you're invisible, Captain."

I played along.

"Where are you, Captain?" Arnold called out, looking around.

"Can't you boys see me?"

The Captain made a face to make us laugh.

We kept quiet.

"Haha!" the Captain said. "I'm invisible! I have to go try this out!"

Then he disappeared.

Juan was outside with his daughter. Juan smokes.

"Ultra-deadly," Arnold said.

Juan was lying out in the sun.

"Now I'll be nice and tan," Juan said.

"Yeah, just like Farmer Brown," we said and left.

Tonight is the county fair. There they burn lots of bons. They call it a bonfire.

Three years ago I saw an extra-nice fire. I was with my cousins Taylor and Claude out in the country. There was lots of good stuff in their basement. Like a box with trash in it.

"A nice bonfire this could be," Taylor said.

"Agreed," I said.

Claude wondered if it wasn't a little *riskatious*.

"Of course not," Taylor said.

"Agreed," I said.

We made a bonfire in the basement. It burned well. Too well. Then there wasn't any good stuff left in the basement. Everything burned up. Taylor and I never confessed. Claude did. He got a prize from the fire department for best tattling. Stupid of me and Taylor not to confess. We regretted it for nineteen minutes. After that we called the fire department about other fires. In case they maybe had any more prizes to give out.

"There's a big fire at the fairgrounds," we informed them.

"We know! It's the annual bonfire," the fire department said and hung up. We didn't get a prize.

One time Arnold and I happened to burn a hole in Dad's pants. He didn't notice until he was at work.

"Pants burn fast," Arnold said.

"So does Dad's fuse," I said when Dad was done yelling at us.

"If you play with fire you're going to get burned," he said.

"If you play with butter you're going to get churned," I said.

Well said. I think it was my sixth sense that helped me out.

I'm going to buy a power drill.

"What do you need a drill for?" Mom asked.

"Just to drill with sometimes and make some holes in the walls."

"Borrow your dad's then," Mom suggested.

"Think if he's loaned it to somebody when I need it . . . and anyways, Dad's drill is pretty nerdy."

"Well you don't need to buy a brand-new drill just to make some holes," Mom nagged.

"But it can be good to have for a little of this and a little of that."

The discussion was closed.

Today on the radio they said that spring was here. I've written a spring poem:

Spring is fine
Love will never be mine
Arnold and I like magic
Mom's bowling is tragic
And Dad just whines.

80

I think that in ten years everybody's car will be able to fly.

Bye-bye apple pie.

May 14

Arnold's mom is dead. Arnold doesn't like it very much. He was sad yesterday. Little Eric and I tried to cheer him up. It didn't work very well. Because Little Eric had an earache. And as for me, I'm a lot worse off than earaches and dead mothers. I've got bad vision. I am a bearer of glasses. I haven't shown my face to anybody. Just to Arnold and Little Eric. They said I looked good in glasses. They lied. Stupid germ-giant. I hid my glasses in my back pocket. Then I sat down on everything I could see. The glasses didn't break. Bad luck.

"Maybe we can make contact with your mom somehow," I told Arnold.

"Like how? Should we bury ourselves underground and talk to a skeleton?" Arnold blubbered.

Little Eric comforted Arnold and said that he knew how it felt.

"My grandma's grandma's uncle is dead, too. I know. . . ."

Arnold shook Little Eric's head for a while.

Then Little Eric and I figured out how we'd get hold of Arnold's dead mom:

1. Go to where she is: the cemetery.

2. Sing a song she liked when she was alive: California Girls.

3. Wait till the grave opens up.

4. Talk to Arnold's mom for a few minutes. Or scream and faint if your name is Little Eric.

It was scary at the cemetery. Little Eric said that he saw the Grim Reaper behind a tree. He was waving at Little Eric.

"Go over and see what he wants then," Arnold said.

Little Eric didn't go. He stayed with us.

"Here it is!" said Arnold. "Here's where my mom is, getting all eaten up by worms."

"How disgusting!" Little Eric said.

"MY MOTHER IS NOT DISGUSTING!" Arnold roared.

Then we sang. I knew almost two whole lines. *I wish they all could be California girls. I wish they all could be California girls.* Little Eric knew one word. *I . . .* Then he just sang *la la la.* Arnold screamed a solo. It sounded nice. Like an airplane.

Our song didn't work. Arnold's mom didn't open her grave. Then Arnold sang a song of his own. Little Eric and I weren't allowed to sing with him. Just to clap the beat.

"Can't you hear what I say, Mom? Come see me today! Hey, hey, is what I say. Don't take the subway, I don't have an X-ray, Mom, Mom hey. Hey, Mom, hey!"

Then we thought we saw the wind blow sort of mysterious-like across the grave.

"Look," Arnold called out. "A dandelion! I know it wasn't here before, I know it! It must have been Mom."

Arnold and I rejoiced. Little Eric didn't. He fainted.

Arnold tried to do CPR. He got Little Eric's face all wet.

Arnold wondered if Little Eric had died. I didn't know. Arnold wondered if we should bury Little Eric. I said I thought we needed a special permit or something. If we buried him, they'd write it on our driver's licenses when we turn sixteen. We didn't want that. We let Little Eric lie there. He woke up after forty-three seconds. Arnold and I got scared.

"Help, he's risen from the dead!" I screamed.

"Run for your life!" Arnold howled.

We ran. Little Eric did, too.

"Wait guys! Come on, quit it," the ghost said.

We held our ears. We ran all the way to Arnold's, and we locked the door. When the ghost started crying outside on the steps we realized that it was Little Eric. We opened the door. Then we ate toasted corn and drank punch.

Toasting corn is fun. You open a can of corn and pour it in the toaster. Wait a minute and then eat. Bon appétit.

Benny in my class has athlete's foot. I'm glad. Our teacher says it's not contagious. I hope she's lying. I need it for tomorrow. Tomorrow we have an important soccer game against the other sixth-grade class, class 6B. We're going to win.

Something else is happening tomorrow. Not fun. I'm being forced to take my awfully dreadful glasses to school. I hope I have time to die before tomorrow.

Bye-bye apple pie.

85

Howdy Doody Uncle Rudy, diary.

Today was one of the worst days ever to exist in the world. Treb Vladinsky was forced to take his new glasses to school.

I got up at 5:30 to test them. First I put them on the tip of my nose. I looked like an owl.

"Hoo hoo," I said to the mirror.

Then I put them on the arch of my nose. I was Vice Principal Berntsim.

Then I put them right up to my eyes. I was a bookworm.

"Awful," I said, and hid my glasses in my glasses case.

"Don't forget your glasses," Mom said after breakfast.

"What glasses?" I said.

"Your nice new ones," Mom said.

"My ugly new ones," I said, and tried to forget where I had put them. I couldn't. They were on my desk.

But then I lost my memory three times. Mom found my glasses every time. Bad luck.

I didn't say anything at school. I left my glasses on the floor in the hall. A good place to get stepped on, I thought hopefully.

During first period it was business as usual.

During second period my teacher kept looking at me.

After the bell rang, she asked me:

"Where are your glasses, Treb?"

During third period we had show-and-tell. Me. I had to have my glasses on the whole time.

During fourth period I kept thinking about a certain tattletale whose name is Mom who squealed to a teacher about her own son. Doesn't family mean *anything* anymore?

In the cafeteria, Nugget met me with a big smile.

"Are those to help you see where to brown-nose?" he hollered.

"Misfit," I mumbled.

"Do you want me to carve you a cane, little blind man?" Nugget went on.

"Why don't you carve your thumb off," I said almost loud enough for him to hear me.

"Glasses, molasses," Nugget howled, "you are *sooooo* ugly!"

I went away.

Arnold was looking for worms by the playground. He had two cans. One with whole worms and one with half ones.

"Food for my frogs," Arnold said.

Arnold told me that you can cure nearsightedness.

"I just need to see how they do it on TV first," he said. "Then we can try it on you."

"How do you do it?" I wondered.

"You cut somewhere behind the eyeball," Arnold explained.

Glasses might not be such a bad thing after all.

After lunch was the soccer season's big opening match. 6A against 6B.

Nugget said that I shouldn't get to play. He said I wouldn't be able to see which goal to shoot in. Everybody else agreed with Nugget. Then I headed the ball eight times and juggled thirty-one times on my right thigh. Everybody was convinced. Nobody wanted to fire me.

In the locker room, all of us in 6A knew we were going to win.

"Piece of cake," Nugget said.

We sang a mean and nasty song:

Sassy lassy pudding grass
No one in 6B can pass
Sassy lassy pudding boot
No one in 6B can shoot
6A! 6A!

6B held their ears.

Nugget took the job of goalie.

"Then you don't have to run," he said.

Nugget is our next-worst goalie. But he's the strongest kid in the class.

We had a cheerleading squad. The girls and Little Eric. Little Eric had the squeakiest voice. Everybody got a headache when he cheered for us. He had to promise to be quiet for the rest of the game and to mix our Kool-Aid for us instead. He did. He mixed two parts Kool-Aid for every one part water.

OUR TEAM
Goalie: Nugget
Fullbacks: Arnold and Jasper
Halfback: Theobald
Forwards: Treb Vladinsky and Benny and Nigel

A strong team.

Benny and I are on the same soccer team in the city league. There they call him Benny Goldfoot. He scores lots of goals.

ACCOUNT OF THE MATCH BETWEEN 6A AND 6B:

6A opened with a strong thirty-two seconds. Then 6B scored.

Nugget threatened to beat up our opponents. It didn't help. After three minutes and five seconds, 6B

89

led two-nothing. Nugget dropped the ball in the goal when he was throwing it to Jasper.

Nugget got mad. "It was Jasper's fault!"

After 3–0 everyone was a forward except for Arnold. He'd found a good spot for worms next to the field.

"Pass it back to me," Nugget yelled at Jasper.

Then it was four-nothing.

Jasper went in to take a shower.

Austin jumped in to take his place and jumped up to head the ball and jumped onto the crossbar. When 6B and the audience had finished laughing, it was time for halftime.

"I've got a strategy," Nugget said.

"Shoot," we said.

"Kick 'em in the shins and fall down in the penalty area so we get penalty shots."

Sixteen seconds into the second half, everybody on our team fell down in the other team's penalty area.

"Nice acting," 6B hollered and made it 5–0.

Theobald had his own whistle. He blew a little tune. He got thrown out of the game.

Arnold dug up six-and-a-half worms. Then we made him play again.

Then came 6–0.

Arnold dropped a worm. Nugget stepped on it on purpose.

"Murderer," Arnold said and left the field. He asked the girls if they wouldn't mind holding his worms for him. They declined.

Nigel got tripped in the other team's penalty area—by me.

We got a penalty shot.

"The referee is always right, but he's really not too bright!" screamed the girls in 6B.

Benny Goldfoot got to take the kick. He missed the ball and sprained two toes.

"Benny Stonefoot," Nugget said.

"Leave me alone," Benny peeped. "As a matter of fact, I tripped on my athlete's foot."

The school nurse came out and took Benny away. I got to take the penalty shot. I scored!

All the girls in our class cheered. It was nice.

I was a hero for forty-eight seconds. Then came 7–1, in favor of 6B.

Nugget tried to move the goal like in ice hockey. It didn't work.

"Idiots, none of you know how to play soccer!" Nugget screamed and stomped away.

Left on our team were me, Austin, and Nigel. Arnold had found another good spot for worms.

We forfeited. Then it's automatically 5–0 for the opponents.

"That was smart," Arnold said. "0–5 is better than 1–7."

Everybody agreed, except for me. My penalty goal got disqualified.

The result of the match between 6A and 6B: 0–5 but really 1–7. Goal by Treb Vladinsky, of course. One red card. Two spoilsports: Nugget and Jasper. Twelve-and-a-half worms dug up by Arnold. Two sprained toes and almost a concussion. And Treb Vladinsky was a hero for forty-eight seconds.

Bye-bye apple pie.

Oh me oh my, diary.

Some revealing information: I know who read my diary. I interrogated the suspected persons. It wasn't Beatrice or Arnold. They gave all the wrong answers to my questions. A few interrogation questions:

1. Can boys keep a diary?

   The suspects' answer: NO!

2. Have you ever seen a boy write in a diary?

   The suspects' answer: NO!

3. Can a moose smoke a pipe and whistle at the same time?

   The suspects' answer:
   Beatrice: NO! Arnold: Doubtful. I'll check.

NOTE! The last question was specially designed to divert suspicion. It can't have been Nugget who read my diary. I know, because I haven't seen any posters around school about *the diary-writer Treb Vladinsky*.

I found out the truth when I interrogated myself. It was me. I had moved my diary when I was cleaning before the party. That's why it was in the wrong place in my drawer. Relief.

I had to fine myself $1.75, of which 83 cents went to taxes.

Another piece of juicy information: the germ-giant seems to have moved—to my shady-looking neighbor Oliver's apartment. I saw him in the window. Oliver, that is. He was wearing glasses. Not sunglasses. The germ-giant has infected him with nearsightedness. Oliver only has himself to blame, you know, as shady-looking as he is.

Arnold and I did some interesting experiments over the weekend. We experimented on Arnold's little sister Doris.

EXPER. (NOTE: abbreviation) 1:

Arnold had a theory that if you drank a drink made with dishwashing detergent, then soap bubbles would bubble out of your mouth when you talked. I didn't believe him. So we had to check—on Doris.

We said it was a health drink. She bought it. Nothing bubbled out of her mouth. But tears ran out of her eyes.

"Interesting side effect," Arnold said.

Doris finished the glass.

"More," she said.

"Obviously addictive," I noted importantly and wrote it into our experiment journal.

Recipe for a dishwashing-detergent drink:

> a pinch of dishwashing detergent,
>   about 1/2 cup
>
> a glass of water
>
> 1 ice cube
>
> Stir. Mix well. Serve and enjoy.

EXPER. 2:

We discovered that if you put a blindfold on a certain person and let that person walk toward a wall, the person will stop automatically just before they get to the wall.

It didn't work on Doris. She walked right into the wall.

"Haven't you ever heard of your sixth sense, Dippy-Doris?" Arnold asked angrily. He tried *his* sixth sense. It worked.

But Arnold looked under the blindfold and saw the wall.

Your sixth sense is an important thing. Certain things are easier to understand. For example, that Dad cheated when he was fasting. My sixth sense told me about that. For example, that our neighbor Oliver Culver is a shady character. My sixth sense told me about that, too. For example, that ambulances have sirens and mailcars don't, so that you won't get them confused. It would look pretty stupid if you got a patient in your mailbox and if a package got tonsillitis. Your sixth sense reveals things like that to you. In some places your sixth sense is stronger than in others. It's weaker at school than at home.

For the second time in my diary I'm going to switch to a red pen.

Now I'm going to write about Nadia.

Nadia is the prettiest name there is. I didn't think so a month ago. But I do now.

Nadia Nelson, class 6E, Mermin Elementary School. I saw Nadia Nelson for the first time on Friday, at the dance at her school. Every week one of the elementary schools has a dance. That's good. I went with Arnold and Theobald. Theobald had mousse in his hair. Ha! Ha! We all had jean jackets on. We were almost a gang.

There are good-looking chicks at Mermin. Some of them even dye their hair. One of the ones who didn't dye her hair was Nadia Nelson. She looked good anyway.

She was dancing with five of her friends.

"Who's that?" I said all tough-like to Arnold and Theobald.

"Nadia Nelson," Theobald said. "She plays the violin in my orchestra."

Theobald told me that Nadia lives out by the soccer fields, in a little house with her mom and her three brothers.

"Her brothers seem like they're pretty barbaric," Theobald said.

Nadia looked at me four times. The fourth time she smiled.

I asked Theobald *how* barbaric her brothers were.

"They're up-and-coming thieves and murderers, probably," he said. The brothers pick Nadia up from music school. They yell out bad words. Sometimes they moon everybody. Her brothers chew tobacco and smoke at the same time. They drive a car and have leather boots and leather jackets with rivets. Their car is an old Mustang, with dice hanging from the rearview mirror and a rug on the ceiling. The brothers punch holes in the top of their car just to show that they have muscles. Then they scream "FOOD FOOD FOOD" and peel out so fast that flames shoot out from their tires.

I was wondering just how dangerous it was to start liking Nadia. It was then that she smiled at me, and made my whole body feel warm.

"Definitely worth the risk," I said.

Nadia has black eyes and dark-brown, curly hair. Sparks jump out wherever she goes.

Oh, diary, when she smiled at me, I wanted to give her a hug and blow in her ears. I didn't. It's hard to blow from twelve feet away.

Arnold and Theobald and I rode our bikes home together.

I was thinking about Nadia the whole time.

Arnold did a wheelie to see if his back fender would hit the pavement. It did.

I hope I'm going to get lots of use out of my red pen. Nadia Nelson—the violinist at Mermin Elementary School.

Tomorrow I'm going to buy a CD single with violin music.

Bye-bye apple pie.

May 22

Kling, klong. Spling, splong, diary.

Now I'm going to write something fun.

I've been brave this week. Several times, even. One brave thing was that I tailed my suspicious neighbor Oliver. He looked almost dangerous. He went in to the LIQUOR STORE! That's where they give out beer and wine and other poison stuff. Then Shady Oliver disappeared . . . into an apartment building. Suspicious. But brave.

Another brave thing was that I wore my glasses at school. Almost all day!

Not even Nugget teased me. Even though he grinned twice.

My teacher said I was brave.

"Of course," I said in a deep voice.

A third brave thing was to make a secret call to Nadia. Nadia Nelson from Mermin Elementary School. The one with the three scary brothers. I called from a phone booth so they couldn't trace my call. It took a long time for me to get ready.

"No, Nadia. I'm that guy you saw on Friday. The one you looked at," I practiced four times.

It didn't sound good.

"Hey, chick. Go to the third bench at Castle Park at three o'clock. Somebody you like will be waiting there for you."

That didn't sound good either.

"This is Treb Vladinsky's automatic babe selection service. You, Nadia Nelson, have been appointed by Treb Vladinsky to become his girlfriend. Please accept after the beep. BEEP!"

I didn't say that.

I wrote everything I wanted to say on a piece of paper. Good thing I was born smart.

Then I lost the piece of paper.

Now for the brave stuff. I called anyway. Nadia's three brothers answered! And I *didn't* hang up.

"Who the heck is it?" said the brothers into the phone.

"Is Nadia in?" I asked as tough as I dared.

The situation was deadly.

"Who is it?" the brothers wanted to know.

"Nobody special," I answered.

"Funny name," said the brothers ominously.

"Is it for me?" somebody in the background asked.

"It's your fiancé!" the brothers roared.

I felt dizzy. But I didn't say anything.

"Hello, this is Nadia," said a voice.

"Hi, my name is . . . Arnold."

Good lie. Arnold sounds better than Treb.

"Hi," Nadia said.

"Uh," I said. "Uh," I said. "Uh," I said.

After the sixth *uh,* Nadia asked me what I wanted.

"Uh," I said. "Is it . . . is it hard to play the violin?"

"Play the violin?" Nadia asked, surprised.

"Another bow-screecher!" screamed the brothers in the background.

"I've gotten interested in violin music. I bought a CD single with violin music yesterday," I lied.

"Oh really?" Nadia said.

"I'm thinking of taking up playing. Do you have any advice?"

"Nadia and Bow-Screecher sitting in a tree . . . ," howled Nadia's three brothers.

"Sorry about my brothers. They're crazy."

"Mmmm," I said.

Then I got dizzy again. What if her brothers had heard me say, "Mmmm?" They'd come run over me with their Mustang. On purpose.

Nadia asked if she knew me.

"We were at the same dance on Friday. We looked at each other four times. I'm Theobald's friend," I said rapidly.

"OK, now I know," Nadia said, and her voice sounded warm and happy.

"It would be fun to get a violin lesson," I said innocently.

"It would be fun to give a violin lesson," Nadia said just as innocently.

"It would be fun to poke a certain person in the eye with a violin bow," the brothers screamed.

"Listen, Arnold," Nadia said into the phone, "why don't we . . . "

Then we were cut off. I had run out of quarters. What rotten luck! I didn't have any more money. It was Dad's fault. If he was rich and a millionaire, I would've put more coins in.

Treb Vladinsky went home. Felt like Jell-O.

Two suspicious persons were creeping around in front of the Mini-Mart. They were about fifteen years old. Treb Vladinsky, more Jell-O.

"Grunt," called out the suspicious persons.

Treb Vladinsky, Jell-O in his whole body. Treb Vladinsky into the Mini-Mart—begged for a squished box of Jell-O mix. Ran home. Thought about Nadia Nelson. Ate all the Jell-O mix straight from the packet.

Mr. Diary. Girls are pretty interesting again.

A fourth brave thing I did was to talk to God about Nadia. Grandma told me that you can wish things from God.

"If you're pleasant and polite, there's no problem," she says.

This is what I did: I put on my nicest clothes, a tie and stuff like that. Then I went up to the biggest window in our apartment so God could see that somebody was there. Then I shined the lamp on my face so that God would recognize me. Then I bowed politely three times. Then I looked pleasant. Then I waved cautiously up at the sky. Then I said:

"Well, God. Do you maybe possibly think that I might be able to go steady with Nadia Nelson? The one with the three dangerous brothers who aren't at all pleasant and polite. Do you think you might be able to arrange it? If so, say YES. Now."

"YES!" God didn't say.

But God blinked a star at me.

"While you're at it, God, you might as well go ahead and get a new car for my dad. A better one than Nugget's. Thanks in advance. Treb Vladinsky says amen and thanks."

I think it worked—as pleasant and polite as I was, with a tie and everything.

There was a civil war in Hoppalochinia yesterday.

There were two leaders, General Arnold and

General Treb. General Arnold shot rubber bands. General Treb shot a squirt gun filled with dye. The war escalated. General Arnold dropped water-bombs on General Treb. Then the U.N.—Mom, that is—arrived. The U.N. said that there were cookies and punch in the kitchen.

There was peace.

We ate peace-cookies and drank peace-punch. The peace-cookies looked like Lisa's boobs. Worth noting.

Bye-bye apple pie.

Hi, diary.

Yippie-ay tra la, hot dogs for us all.

That was a rhyme. Rhymes are fun. Some more fun rhymes:

Eat a moose—rinse with juice.
Don't harass—Dad has gas.
Nugget is a moron—can't get his shoes on.
AND
Nadia Nelson is a good-looking chick—
she gives me the hick-ups, HICK!
(NOTE: This one is new.)

Dad is trying to grow a beard.

Poor Mom! He looks like a criminal, who does murders and everything.

"Dad, you've got some dirt on your chin," I say.

"Yeah, well, it's called a beard," Dad growls.

I've stopped taking showers. I blame it all on my beard.

"Wash your hands, Treb," Mom nags.

"I can't. It's a beard," I say and look at Dad.

We talked about the future at school today.

"In the future, everything will be older," I said.

"Explain yourself," my teacher asked.

I mumbled something to myself and didn't say any more.

Sharon is going to be a TV anchorwoman.

"I hope you don't drown when they throw you overboard," Nugget said and laughed for about four minutes and eleven seconds. Then he said:

"In a year it's just gonna be BOOM, PLATCH, KRUNCH, and atomic bombs and world war. We're all going to die."

Three people started crying.

"And CHOFF and SPLICH and KERSPLUNCH," Nugget went on, jumping up and down.

He got a free ticket to the principal's office.

Arnold had a theory. He said that the Earth would be square since first it was flat and then it was round.

He went up to the chalkboard and showed us what it'd be like.

"I'll do some tests. I'll get back to you with the results," Arnold said and sat down.

Raphaela is going to be a housewife and marry a rich old man.

"My dad is single," Arnold said.

"Is he rich?" Raphaela asked.

"No, but he plays the lottery."

"What songs does he know?" Nigel yelled out.

The whole class laughed. Then we got expelled.

Now on to the thriller about Nadia Nelson and the three brothers. In the last episode, our hero Treb Vladinsky made a call from a phone booth. Risking his life. The three brothers' scary attempts to shorten Treb Vladinsky's conversation failed.

Treb Vladinsky used the code name Arnold.

Treb Vladinsky and Nadia Nelson almost made a date for going violining. Then the coins in the pay phone ran out.

Treb Vladinsky made some inquiries among the general public about Nadia Nelson. The general public was Theobald. This is the information he was able to gather:

She was born in the fall and in West Virginia.

She's good at the violin.

Her brothers drive rapidly through town at night— in a car of the brand Mustang.

Their chimney is full of soot.

Nadia's favorite food: spaghetti and meat sauce. (Good thing it's not mushroom stew.)

She ties her left shoelace first.

Obvious conclusion about Nadia Nelson: She is Treb Vladinsky's absolutely most favorite girl.

Obvious conclusion about her brothers: They're deadly.

Treb Vladinsky has hired a spy. Theobald—with a license to snoop. Theobald is in the same orchestra as Nadia Nelson. They're *just* friends. Theobald is busy with Raphaela. Good.

End of the thriller about Nadia Nelson and the three brothers.

Right now I'm preparing myself for a difficult and gruesome task. I'm going to call Nadia again. Not from home, of course. Mom and Dad would tease me to death.

I've written down all my important questions on a piece of paper.

I've filled my pockets with quarters.

I've combed my hair and cut my nails.

I wonder if God was listening when we chatted about Nadia. I hope it helped. If it didn't, then maybe next time I'll have to try standing outside and talking. Someone's coming . . .

Someone was Dad. He didn't see anything. It was a close call. Dad wanted his adjustable wrench and his screwdriver back. I've been using them as drumsticks in my new rock band. We're going to perform on the last day of school and lip-synch. Two girls are going to sing backup and dance. Raphaela and Sharon. Sharon thinks that an adjustable wrench is also called a twistie-bar. She's crazy. But she's a good dancer.

Arnold really wanted Madelyn to sing backup. Since he thought that Madelyn was in *amour* with him. She wasn't. Arnold was sad. He bit Madelyn on the arm during our quiet-reading time. Then it wasn't quiet. Madelyn cried and Arnold barked like a bulldog.

Bye-bye apple pie.

Sunday the 31st of May

Hoo-hoo moo-moo, diary.

Today, once again, I'm going to do most of my writing in red. Reason, of course, Nadia Nelson.

I made phone call number two on Tuesday. This happened:

The brothers didn't answer.

Nadia answered. Her voice was soft and sweet.

"Do you remember last time?" I asked.

"Who is this?" she asked.

"Ne . . . Tre . . . Arnold," I said.

My code name is still Arnold.

"I didn't have enough coins last time," I explained.

"That's OK."

Then we talked about violin strings and stuff like that for three minutes and twelve seconds. I asked Nadia if she was going to go to the dance on Friday.

"Well, my Mom and I are probably going to bake some bread together," she said.

All hope was gone.

"I'm thinking of going," I said desperately.

"Well, you know, bread isn't really all that important," Nadia said quickly.

"Maybe we'll see each other there," I said almost tough-like.

"Could be," said Nadia.

A roar was heard in the background. It was Nadia's brothers. Returned from cruising the town.

"Food!" they screamed.

Nadia and I said a pretty quick good-bye.

On Friday it was time for the dance. I got dressed up in sort of violin clothes.

"What a handsome son," Mom said.

Theobald, Arnold, and I were a gang again when we got to the dance. Arnold bought a bag of popcorn and stuffed a kernel up his nose. Our whole rock band was there.

Theobald plays a high-hat cymbal. One. Flutes are nerdy in rock bands. I play professional drums, and Little Eric maybe plays the accordion. Or the tambourine if he can't borrow the accordion from his dad. Jasper plays heavy-metal guitar. It sounds like a tractor when he pulls on the strings. Sharon and Raphaela dance and act stupid. Arnold has never heard a whole song. He's the electrician. No one was dancing yet so the whole band sat down at a table and discussed our first gig on the last day of school. Little

Eric told us that the principal wanted a name for our band for all the posters.

"How about using our school name? The Bessemer Dudes," Jasper suggested.

"Two of us are actually dud*ettes,* you know," Sharon said.

"Mama's Dwarves," I said, but instantly got out-voted.

Raphaela thought for one and a half minutes. Then she said:

"Head Over Heels."

"Are you a raving lunatic?" I asked.

"Yes!" Arnold screamed. "That'll be our name."

Now we're called the Raving Lunatics.

"Too bad we can't play for real," Theobald said.

"We're lucky," I said. "With Arnold as an electrician, it's a good thing we're only lip-synching. Otherwise everything would catch on fire."

There was a popcorn war. Arnold almost got thrown out.

Then Nadia came.

She was pretty.

I whispered to Theobald to go snoop some. Theobald went over to Nadia and snooped some.

After a few minutes Nadia looked at Arnold! And then at me. The whole thing was mysterious. Theobald came back while Arnold was buying more popcorn. So I asked:

"What did Nadia say?"

"She wondered what your name was."

"So what did you say?"

"*Ned,* of course," Theobald said.

Oh, no! My geeky, nerdy, real name had been exposed. No girl could ever like a guy named Ne . . . I mean, *Treb.* The whole world fell to pieces. The walls crumbled and somewhere twenty wolves howled. Treb Vladinsky was alone—again.

Then our rock band snuck into the school's music room and counted guitars. When we were finished, Arnold suggested we go back to the dance and cruise for girls.

"Good idea," everybody said except me.

I had cruised enough.

"Watch out, foxy ladies," Arnold said in the hall.

But they didn't have to watch out. The dance was over. Everybody had gone home. Treb Vladinsky didn't go with the rest of the gang to watch a movie at Nigel's. Treb Vladinsky ran home to prepare for the *final test!* A last and crucial call to Nadia.

Dad and Larry Fotzwit were playing cards. They let me play. We played bullsh . . . bull-pudding until one o'clock. Dad lost. He got the most pudding. Then came Larry and I was the best, of course.

Larry Fotzwit lives in the apartment up and over from us. He works with computers and he knows what a TV looks like on the inside. Otherwise he's just like a normal man. Except that he's forgetful sometimes. For example, twice he thought we were playing poker.

Last fall he forgot that he was supposed to fly to Miami on vacation. His daughter Arlene reminded him, the day after.

"Oh yeah," Larry said and hitchhiked to Canada.

Bulletin about Saturday morning. The *final test*. The third and last try. The call to Nadia Nelson.

Place: The phone booth in front of the bike shop.

Time: 10:53:16

RING.

"What do you want?" answered Nadia's three brothers.

Maximal bad luck! Everything started out wrong.

"Is Nadia not available?" I asked.

"How'd you guess, pie-for-brains?" said the oldest brother, whose name Theobald said was Mick.

"Is it her secret lover?" shouted the next-oldest brother, whose name was Meck.

Then there was a *crash* somewhere.

"What was that?" I asked.

"Oh, it was just Moreland dropping the TV on the floor."

Moreland is the youngest and deadliest.

After a while a beautiful voice floated through the phone.

"Is it for me?"

"Is it for me?" the brothers mimicked.

The moment had arrived. My whole future was at stake.

"This is Nadia," said Nadia.

"Hey! It's Tr . . . Arnold." I almost gave myself away.

"Yeah, hi, Arnold," Nadia interrupted. "There's something I have to tell you. Yesterday at the disco when I saw you guys, Theobald showed me who was who. And the truth of the matter is, that I'm in love . . . "

"Yipp," I whispered into the phone.

"With *Ned!*"

It was quiet for one minute. My brain spun around in my head and wanted to fly away. I almost fainted a few times. What should I say? After all, I'd told her my name was Arnold. And Nadia didn't want to talk to me because she thought I was Arnold, since she's in love with Treb, who is me, when I'm not Arnold.

"Then you're in love with me," I said quietly into the phone.

"Huh?" Nadia said.

"Then you're in love with me!" I screamed.

"Hahaha," the brothers laughed and I started to sweat.

"Don't say that, Arnold," Nadia said and sounded sad.

"But . . . ," I said.

"I'm really in love with *Ned,*" Nadia said and hung up.

This is crazy. How am I ever going to be able to . . .

Darn! Mom just screamed for the sixth time that dinner's ready. I have to go now.

Bye-bye apple pie.

June 1, this year

Diary!

Everything in life wants to laugh at Treb Vladinsky and tweek his ears.

Love has sprouted wings and flown away from me. It's flying to Japan to land on a Japanese person instead.

Nadia will never be mine.

The reason: the masquerade catastrophe.

The masquerade catastrophe took place at the masquerade yesterday. Arnold, Little Eric, and I decided to go to this week's elementary school dance. I wanted to meet Nadia to tell her that I'm not Arnold, I'm Treb, and that Arnold was Arnold and *not* Treb. Because that's me.

"Sorry, muchachos," said the teacher at the door. "This is a masquerade. You're not dressed up."

Arnold lied and said he was dressed up as a guy named Arnold. I tried to make myself look fat and like a doughnut with whipped cream in my hair. Little Eric almost got in. He looks like plankton.

We went home and changed. We were in a hurry, so we had to take whatever clothes we could find.

Arnold became my mom, I became a mini-dad, and Little Eric was a pink bunny rabbit.

Me, Mom, and the bunny took off for the masquerade. The teacher at the door asked Arnold for a slow-dance.

Inside the cafeteria-turned-disco, the music pounded. The lights blinked. Arnold thought something was wrong with the electrical system. Bunny Eric got a migraine from all the blinking.

Nugget was there. Unfortunately. He was dressed up as a monster.

"Aren't you supposed to be dressed up?" I didn't say. I said:

"Cool."

"I know," Nugget answered. "But you're not."

The conversation was over. So was Little Eric. He was gone.

"Where'd he go?" I asked Arnold.

Arnold didn't know. He was gone, too.

It didn't matter. I was supposed to be finding Nadia. I saw her, far far far away—at least three miles and four feet away. In a life-size scale. Nadia had a pretty disguise. She was a redneck with a tattoo on her arm. I was going to go over and charm her. But I got nervous and my forehead got sweaty. I wanted to wipe off all the sweat with a paper towel. I walked toward the bathroom. A pink bunny hopped by.

"Little Eric," I said. "Come on into the bathroom."

Little Eric didn't want to. He acted silly and looked scared. I pulled him in.

I showed Little Eric my thirteen different ways to pee. Here are a few:

Holding my hands behind my head. And like a dog. Peeing sideways and straight up. Writing my name with the spray. Jumping up and down at the same time. And so on, and so on.

Little Eric was so impressed that he couldn't get out a single word.

"Not bad, eh?" I bragged. "A real pee-pee superstar."

The pee-pee superstar and Little Eric exited the bathroom. Then a girl in a Dr. Seuss hat came up to us. I got ready to turn on the charm. The girl started to talk. But not to me.

"Where have you been, Kate?"

I had no clue what was going on. The girl was calling Little Eric Kate. Little Eric answered in a girlie voice:

"This sicko guy dragged me into the boys' bathroom. And do you know what he did?"

I didn't get to find out what I did. I ran away and hid. Behind a dancing melon and a pirate.

Then Little Eric walked by in his pink bunny outfit. I yelled at him for three minutes and eighteen seconds.

I said that he'd disgraced me. Little Eric apologized. Everything was forgotten. We were friends again.

Now I had to find Nadia. I found Nadia. She was talking to a pink bunny and a girl in a Dr. Seuss hat. They were laughing. It was the end of me. I wanted to sneak home. It didn't work. I was identified by Kate the pink bunny.

"Look! There's the pee-pee superstar!" she hollered out and pointed at me.

It was even more the end of me.

I pretended the bunny was pointing at Nugget.

Then I pretended to dance with a giraffe. I danced toward the exit and snuck outside. The giraffe had to take care of itself.

I danced home and hid in bed. I hope no one finds me.

Now Nadia knows that my name isn't Arnold. My name is Pee-Pee Superstar. Stupid Little Eric.

Now I have to stop writing. I'm going to force Mom and Dad to move us to Japan.

Bye-bye apple pie.

Tuesday, June 2

Yippee yippee yea, diary.

Today everything is best.
Treb Vladinsky is happy.
On Sunday everything was dark.
Today everything is light.
After my unsuccessful conversation with Nadia and my incredible goof at the masquerade, the whole world went to pieces.

Nadia said she loved a boy named Treb. That's me. But she thought my name was Arnold. Because that's what I'd said—as a disguise. But, of course, my name is really Treb. So in other words, Nadia is *in love with me!* Nadia hung up and I ate lunch and then there was the masquerade with Mr. Pee-Pee Superstar and all that.

I felt sorry for me. And rightly so. I had no idea how to explain all this to Nadia.

Then came the surprise. I got orders from Mom.

"Go buy flowers for Aunt Trish because she's in the hospital again."

"Thank you," I said and left.

It's not un-dangerous to buy flowers.

The way there was calm.

On the way back it happened.

Nadia Nelson was eating an ice cream cone under the tunnel.

I wanted to run away. I knew Nadia would laugh at me and think my name was Pee-Pee Superstar. Nadia didn't laugh at me. She smiled at me.

"Oh," I said.

"Oh," Nadia said.

"Hi," I said.

"Hi," Nadia said.

"It's a good thing it's not raining," I said.

"Yeah," Nadia said.

"Even though it wouldn't matter if it was raining. Since we're standing under the tunnel."

We laughed in synch. My head pounded. I felt foggy.

"Here are some flowers for you," I said and forgot about Aunt Trish.

"Oh, thank you," Nadia said in surprise. "What are these for?"

I didn't answer. I just grinned all silly-like.

Nadia understood.

Everything felt wonderful.

Then Nadia did that thing. She ran her hand across my cheek! I almost called for help with happiness. We stood quiet for a minute and looked at each other. A howl was heard.

"That's my brothers," Nadia said. "I have to go."

A deathly scary situation. Three dangerous brothers on the approach. Under the road, the forbidden couple.

"Can we meet?" I whispered quickly.

"Huh, hurry. Home! *Food!*" the savages screamed along the way.

"Sure, but not at my house, OK?"

The forbidden couple made a date for neutral territory. Without her brothers or Arnold.

"I have to go on a field trip with the orchestra after school tomorrow. But I'll be home on Thursday."

"Me, too. For sure."

"Our corn dogs're waiting! Fast, fast, fast!" the brothers howled from the car.

"By the old oak in Castle Park at four o'clock," Nadia said and ran off.

"Pleasant," Treb Vladinsky said and sailed home on clouds. Happy.

"Where are the flowers for Aunt Trish?" Mom asked.

"You won't believe it, but I was robbed!" I whispered.

"Robbed?!" Mom screamed.

I pressed out three tears to make it look real.

"Yeaaah," I cried. "By some kind of gang."

"And they took all your money?" Mom asked, horrified.

"No, they took the *flowers,*" I told her and pressed out two new tears.

I had to describe how they looked. Then Dad went out to look for some kind of gang with newly stolen flowers. He couldn't find them. Good thing.

I can't wait for my date on Thursday.

Yesterday we had a cleaning day at school. We picked up trash. I found four good things. Arnold found tons. My good things:

a wrench to take the cleats off of cleats

prank article no. 33: fake chewing gum

four living beetles

half a broomstick

"Here's the biggest piece of trash," Nugget said and tried to stuff Benny into the trash can.

Arnold counted blades of grass. He got to 2,394. Then he lost track. Theobald found a hockey puck that he tried to sell. No one bought it. Raphaela got stuck in a thorn bush. Her cheek bled.

"First-class entertainment," Nugget said happily.

After we'd finished cleaning I held a spy meeting with Theobald.

"Keep an eye on Nadia during the field trip," I said. "Save her from all the guys."

Theobald promised. The meeting was adjourned. Friends are a good thing to have. And not all that expensive either. Theobald wanted four dollars. He got $2.50.

Thank-you speech to God. To be communicated only in this manner:

Thank you God for the encounter with Nadia. Slick move, using the tunnel like that. If you need my services some time, just let me know. Otherwise no requests. Thank you and amen and all that.

Soon we're going to get out of school. During summer vacation I'm going to collect aluminum cans and make money.

We're going on vacation. To Asia. NOTE: Lie.

We're going to the beach. The beach is on the side of the country. Good to know if you get lost.

I've written a new chapter of *Cowboy-Kurt*:

Cowboy-Kurt was extra strong and brave. His good friend, the inventor Arnold von Otto, invented green hair. Then the thug Nasty Nuggy came along and swiped the formula for green hair. Von Otto called on Cowboy-Kurt.

"I'm somewhat very angry," said the inventor curtly. "The formula was important for everybody's survival."

Cowboy-Kurt found Nasty Nuggy in some sort of a warehouse. The thug had two pistols and was planning to burn up the formula with fire. It started to burn. Then Cowboy-Kurt woke up. It was all a dream. The end.

But Nadia Nelson is no dream.

Bye-bye apple pie.

Thursday, June 4

Good day, burned-up diary.

Unlucky that I have a friend named Arnold.

Unlucky that he wanted to do an experiment on you, diary! Especially unlucky that he set fire to all the empty pages except this one—in the name of science.

Arnold wanted to check something.

"I have to see if the paper in your diary burns as fast as the paper in mine."

"*You keep a diary, too?*" I asked in surprise.

"Yeah, that's where I write down all my formulas and certain top-secret drawings."

Then there was a *Fssshhhhhhh!*

"Talk about a turbo-diet," Arnold said and pointed at my burned-up diary. "It took ten seconds," he continued and wrote down the time in his own burned-up diary.

Interesting that there can be found two males in the same area who are secret diary-writers.

Since this is the last page of my skull-and-crossbones diary, I feel like I should give some kind of conclusion to the rest of the book. Certain stupid parts will be excluded.

First something about the neighbors: Juan Bergstrom bought a house out in the woods.

"We're going to get fourteen pigs," Juan said.

"Perfect for somebody as pig-headed as you are," I said and got chased around the block.

Juan's wife is going to have a new baby. Kind of like you have someone over for dinner. But for longer.

"If it's a girl we're going to name her Matilda. If it's a boy we're going to name him King," Juan says.

I think he's lying.

The Captain, in the apartment on the bottom right, shot himself in the foot. He was cleaning his rifles.

"An old injury from the war!" he hollered from the ambulance.

"What war?" I asked him.

"WWI," the Captain said.

They stuck him with a needle and he went to sleep.

My suspicious-looking neighbor Oliver Culver has been removed from the suspicious list. I tailed him. He bought me an ice cream cone and juggled his shoes. People who juggle their shoes aren't dangerous.

Old Lady Andersen thinks that Larry Fotzwit across the hall is trying to poison her to death.

"He smokes in the stairwell because he wants

me to get the Sooty-Lung disease," Old Lady Andersen whines. "And besides, he leaves dirty, bacteria-producing boots outside his door."

And so my last neighbors: Larry Fotzwit and his daughter Arlene. Larry locked himself out six times in two weeks—a new record! Another time he forgot he lived behind the door on the right. He tried to break into Old Lady Andersen's on the left. The police came. Larry Fotzwit is more fun than Santa Claus.

Two nice things: Nugget is moving to Sioux Falls and the germ-giant was found dead in the trash bin outside. Or was it the other way around? NOTE: funny joke.

Something sad: Hoppalochinia is no more. The country has ceased to exist. There was a nuclear war between General Treb and General Arnold. Negotiations broke down. Hoppalochinia was erased from the Earth's surface. The generals survived.

"Unpleasing," General Arnold said.

Our rock band practiced day before yesterday. We learned how to bow for the show on the last day of school. We had special-ordered two applauders from the third grade.

Little Eric was super-nervous. First he curtsied

instead of bowing. When everybody was finished laughing we started over.

When we were supposed to try it again, Little Eric couldn't take the pressure. Ten minutes later Nigel had to drag him out of the bathroom. Then he bowed onto the cymbal and made his forehead bleed. One of the applauders left.

We special-trained Little Eric for four minutes. The applauder came back and thought that Little Eric had some kind of jack-in-the-box disease.

We practiced our bowing for forty minutes and our songs for nine.

"Oh, by the way, our part of the show has landed in the danger zone," I said.

"WHAT?" everybody screamed.

"The teachers have found out that Arnold is our electrician. They might not want to take the risk."

"Slander. I'm a qualified specialist at electrical things and stuff," Arnold said and flipped some switches. Then the electricity went out.

𝄞

My diary is almost finished. Thanks to Arnold.

Now I'm going to write about the most important thing there is.

A book is a life. My life is Nadia.

So I'm going to conclude this book by writing about Nadia Nelson from Mermin Elementary School.

The following happened on the historic Thursday, June 4, by the old oak tree in Castle Park. Time: 4:00 P.M. Treb Vladinsky's arrival: 3:30. Reason: Beautification of the meeting place. I wanted to make a good impression on Nadia. So I took away some trash around the old oak tree and pulled up uneven blades of grass and removed ugly stones and pebbles and kicked away dog poop.

After that I did a silly romantic thing. I carved the initials N. N. in a heart on the trunk of the old oak tree. Fully visible.

3:50 saw the arrival of N. N., in other words Nadia Nelson, in other words the cutest girl in the world, in other words Treb Vladinsky's secret love.

I began romantically:

"The weather is nicer today than last time."

Nadia smiled and nodded.

I fainted inside.

"Do you want to sit down for a minute?" I managed to say.

Nadia smiled and nodded.

Faint number two.

We sat approximately five inches away from each other. Too great a distance, I thought.

"I think I'll move a little," I said. "I'm sitting on a termite hole."

"Poor termite," Nadia said.

Then we were sitting approximately three inches away from each other.

Nadia saw the heart with the N. N. in it.

"I wonder what that means?" she said.

"Maybe . . . N . . . Noisy Nacho?"

Nadia laughed.

"Do you really think so?"

"No," I said and looked at her.

She looked back.

"Think if it means Nadia Nelson," she said.

My ears got warm.

"It does," I said and became a relative of the tomato.

Then we were sitting approximately two inches away from each other.

The moment of truth had arrived.

Nadia stood up and carved the initials N. F. inside the heart, right under N. N.!

"And what does that mean?" I was barely able to say.

"Maybe . . . Neon Fruit," Nadia said.

"Do you really think so?" I asked, floating lightly.

"No," said Nadia. "It means Ned Floyd."

"Oh really," I said and flew away.

Then we were sitting zero inches away from each other.

Nadia ruffled my hair. I was going to ruffle her hair, too, but I accidentally poked her in the eye instead.

"Ow," Nadia said.

"I'm sorry!" I screamed and felt like a murderer.

Nadia said it didn't matter.

We looked at each other again.

After a while I said:

"Nadia is a pretty name."

"So is Ned," Nadia said.

I laughed for thirty seconds.

"Why are you laughing?" Nadia asked.

"I thought you were kidding," I said.

"I really think Ned is a nice name and I really think Ned is nice."

I think I got a fever. We kissed.

Dearest Mr. Diary.

Treb Vladinsky no longer exists.

Now there is only Ned Floyd and Nadia Nelson.

Bye-bye in-love pie.

GAYLORD RG